100 YEARS OF
CATHOLIC SOCIAL TEACHING
DEFENDING
WORKERS & THEIR UNIONS

Summaries & Commentaries
for Five Landmark Papal Encyclicals

JOE HOLLAND

PACEM IN TERRIS PRESS

The Publishing Service of
PAX ROMANA
Catholic Movement for Intellectual & Cultural Affairs
USA

Pax Romana / Catholic Movement for Intellectual & Cultural Affairs - USA
is the United States intellectual-professional federation
of the global Pax Romana Catholic lay movement
of intellectuals, professionals, and university students.

This book is published with gratitude to
Paulist Press for permission to reproduce summaries of
RERUM NOVARUM and QUADRAGESIMO ANNO
from Joe Holland's earlier book
MODERN CATHOLIC SOCIAL TEACHING:
THE POPES CONFRONT THE INDUSTRIAL AGE 1740-1958,
to Sr. Claudia Carlin and Pierian Press for earlier permission to use
papal quotations from Sr. Carlin's multivolume edited collection titled
THE PAPAL ENCYCLICALS;
to UNITE HERE for the cover photo.
All biblical citations are taken from
THE NEW AMERICAN BIBLE.
Note that the non-inclusive language found in quotations from
papal encyclicals does not reflect the preference of the author.

Published by Pax Romana/Cmica-usa
Printed by CreateSpace

ISBN-13: 978-1477467404
ISBN-10: 1477467408

PAX ROMANA
Catholic Movement for Intellectual & Cultural Affairs
USA
1025 Connecticut Avenue NW. Suite 1000
Washington DC 20036
http://paxromanausa.org

ABOUT THE AUTHOR

JOE HOLLAND, an eco-social philosopher and Catholic theologian, holds a Ph.D. in Theology in the field of Social Ethics from the University of Chicago, and was a Fulbright Scholar in Philosophy at the *Universidad Católica* in Santiago, Chile. He is Professor of Philosophy & Religion at Saint Thomas University in Miami Gardens, Florida; Permanent Visiting Professor at the *Universidad Nacional del Altiplano* in Peru; a frequent lecturer at the *Universidad Mayor de San Andrés* in Bolivia;  President of Pax Romana / Catholic Movement for Intellectual & Cultural Affairs USA; co-founder and Vice-Chair of Catholic Scholars for Worker Justice; a member of the Catholic Labor Network; and a member of the International Association for Catholic Social Thought, based at the University of Leuven in Belgium.

Earlier, Joe served as an Associate at the Center of Concern, an internationally oriented social-justice 'think tank' in Washington DC jointly founded by the international Jesuit order and the U.S. Catholic Bishops. While at the Center, he co-founded the National Conference on Religion and Labor, co-sponsored by the AFL-CIO, and he also founded the American Catholic Lay Network. Later, he served as founding Director of the Pallottine Institute for Lay Leadership and Research at Seton Hall University in South Orange, New Jersey. In addition, he was the principal consultant-writer for the 1975 pastoral letter from the 25 Catholic bishops of Appalachia, THIS LAND IS HOME TO ME, and for the 1995 sequel pastoral document AT HOME IN THE WEB OF LIFE.

Joe has lectured at Georgetown, Harvard, Notre Dame, Princeton, and other universities in the United States, as well as at the *Institut Catholique* in Paris, France, Sophia University in Tokyo, Japan, the Pontifical Catholic University in São Paulo, Brazil, the *Universidad Mayor de San Andres* in La Paz, Bolivia, and other universities across the world. In 1986 he was awarded the Isaac Hecker Award for Social Justice, and in 2002 he was awarded the Athena Medal of Excellence by the *Universidad Nacional del Altiplano* in Peru. He is married to Paquita Biascoechea-Martinez Holland, and they have two children and four grandchildren.

PACEM IN TERRIS BOOKS

Promoting Authentically Postmodern Catholic Ecological,
Social, and Spiritual Thought in Service of the Emerging Global Civilization
and the Emerging World Church

THE "POISONED SPRING" OF ECONOMIC LIBERTARIANISM
Menger, Mises, Hayek, Rothbard: A Critique from
Catholic Social Teaching of the Austrian School of Economics
Angus Sibley, 2011

100 YEARS OF CATHOLIC SOCIAL TEACHING
DEFENDING WORKERS & THEIR UNIONS
Summaries & Commentaries for Five Landmark Papal Encyclicals
Joe Holland, 2012

FORTHCOMING

SOCIAL ANALYSIS II
Reading the Signs of the Times for Society and Church
at the End of the Modern World
(Pacem in Terris Global Initiative Volume 1)
Joe Holland, 2012

THE PROPHETIC VISION OF JOHN XXIII
Founder of Catholic Social Teaching for
the Postmodern Global Era, 1958-1963
(Postmodern Catholic Social Teaching, Volume 1)
Joe Holland, Projected for 2012

GLOBAL CAPITALISM IN HISTORICAL CONTEXT
The Local, National, and Global Stages of Modern Western Industrial Capitalism
and the Turbulent Transition to a Postmodern Global Ecological Civilization
(Pacem in Terris Global Initiative Volume 2)
Joe Holland, Projected for 2012

Scholars interested in submitting a related manuscript to be considered for
publication in this Series, should send an email of inquiry to:

pax-romana-cmica-usa@comcast.net

EARLIER BOOKS BY JOE HOLLAND

HUMANITY'S AFRICAN ROOTS
Remembering the Ancestors' Wisdom
2008

BEYOND THE DEATH PENALTY
The Development in Catholic Social Teaching
Co-Editor Michael McCarron
2007

MODERN CATHOLIC SOCIAL TEACHING
The Popes Confront the Industrial Age, 1740-1958
2003

THE NEW DIALOGUE OF CIVILIZATIONS
Co-Editor Roza Pati
2003

THE EARTH CHARTER
A Study Book of Reflection for Action
Co-Author Elisabeth Ferrero
2002

VARIETIES OF POSTMODERN THEOLOGY
Co-Editors David Griffin & William Beardslee
1989

CREATIVE COMMUNION
Toward a Spirituality of Work
1989

AMERICAN AND CATHOLIC
The New Debate
Co-Editor Anne Barsanti
1988

THE VOCATION AND MISSION OF THE LAITY
Co-Author Robert Maxwell
1986

SOCIAL ANALYSIS
Linking Faith and Justice
Co-Author Peter J. Henriot SJ
1980 & 1983

THE AMERICAN JOURNEY
1976

This book is dedicated to

ÓSCAR ARNULFO ROMERO Y GALDÁMEZ

Archbishop of San Salvador, 1977-1980,

a prophetic episcopal leader martyred on 24 March 1980,

for his evangelical defense of the dignity and lives of workers and their families

in his native country of El Salvador.

"The Spirit of the Lord is upon me;

therefore, he has anointed me.

He has sent me to bring glad tidings to the poor,

to proclaim liberty to captives,

recovery of sign to the blind

and release to prisoners,

to announce a year of favor from the Lord."

THE GOSPEL ACCORDING TO LUKE

CHAPTER 4, VERSES 18-19

The repeated calls issued within the Church's social doctrine, beginning with Rerum Novarum, for the promotion of workers' associations that can defend their rights must therefore be honored today even more than in the past, as a prompt and far-sighted response to the urgent need for new forms of cooperation at the international level, as well as the local level.

Benedict XVI
CARITAS IN VERITATE
(Par. 25)

TABLE OF CONTENTS

INTRODUCTION

Crisis of Catholic Evangelization of the Working Classes in Late Modern Global Industrial Capitalism

T oday in the United States (and elsewhere), some Catholic Christians (and some other Christians) have strong hostility toward workers trying to organize themselves into a union, belonging to a union, or defending their union against attacks.

Such class hostility and sometimes even class hatred – no doubt unintentionally but nonetheless effectively – undermines Catholic *solidarity* and *evangelization* of the working classes within late modern Industrial Capitalism.[1] It also rejects over 100 years of Catholic Social Teaching in defense of workers and their unions, and the prophetic Biblical foundations for this defense.[2]

---

[1] In this book, I will capitalize certain words to emphasize their centrality to the debate within and surrounding Catholic Social Teaching. This will include, for example, Capitalism (as well as Industrial Capitalism and Liberal Capitalism), Socialism (or Scientific Socialism), Science, and Technology.

[2] The central narrative of the Hebrew TORAH is the story in the BOOK OF EXODUS of the LORD's *liberation* of the Children of Israel from being unjustly bound in slave-labor by the Pharaoh of Egyptian Empire. This is the deep Biblical root of Liberation Theology, which was the primary Theology of Jesus as

Unjust Class Prejudice against Workers' Unions

Today, such hostility against workers' unions constitutes *an unjust bourgeois class prejudice* against workers and their human rights. Those who carry this prejudice – presumably without realizing it – would deny full human rights to workers. In practice denying workers human rights, they *implicitly* deny workers' humanity.

In response, some may say that they are not against workers and their rights, but only against *unions*. Yet unions are workers who have organized themselves to defend their rights and to participate in collective bargaining.

So any claim that unions are something apart from workers is not true. That false claim is like arguing that the organization known as the Knights of Columbus is separate from its members.

Of course, *some* leaders in labor institutions can become corrupt, just as *some* leaders in business, educational, political, and religious institutions can also become corrupt. But the proper response to corrupt institutional leaders anywhere is not to *destroy* their institutions. Rather, it is to help to *reform* the institutions through promotion of non-corrupt leaders.

---

portrayed in the Gospel of Mark (probably the oldest of the Christian Gospels). The mainstream forms of Liberation Theology are not rooted in Marxism, as some have erroneously claimed. Rather, Marxism (founded by Karl Marx, a secularized Jew who was the direct descendant of prestigious Polish Rabbis going back to the time of Thomas Aquinas) is itself a misguided secularization of the TORAH's divinely inspired liberation narrative of messianic hope. The Exodus of the Children of Israel represents *the first labor strike in recorded history* – again, one divinely inspired and one leading to a more just social order within human history. In this liberation, the LORD of the Bible makes a "preferential option for the poor." All disciples of Jesus are called to this "option."

By the way, while the effects of original sin are presumably shared equally among leaders, it seems important to note that normally leaders of unions are *democratically elected* from and by the other members of their unions. That is not typically the case with the leaders of most other major institutions, outside of politics.

Also, we do not prejudicially presume that *most* leaders in business, education, politics, and religion are bad. Unless proven otherwise, we presume that most of these leaders are well intentioned and are trying to provide ethical leadership.

So why should some people automatically presume that union leaders are bad? Yet, for example, some journalists regularly disparage union leaders by labeling them in the press as *"union bosses."* But they do not use the same *derogatory* language for leaders of other institutions.

Unless proven otherwise, we are obliged in justice to presume that most union leaders are well intentioned and are trying to provide ethical leadership for their *legitimate* institutions.

Blocking Jesus' Evangelical Message

When Catholic Christians succumb to the unjust bourgeois class prejudice against workers' unions – even unintentionally and unconsciously – they *block* the Catholic Church's preaching of Jesus' message of *solidarity* as God's unconditional love for all humans as children of God.

Catholic Social Teaching has made clear that this means that all human persons are endowed by their Creator with God-given human rights, including the right to form associations like workers' unions.

Also, when Catholic Christians fall prey to this bourgeois class prejudice against unions, they also *block* the Holy Spirit's guidance of the Church community toward evangelizing the working classes. Their prejudice then undermines *evangelization.*

Sadly, some leaders of Catholic institutions – primary and secondary schools, colleges and universities, and healthcare and other charitable organizations – do maintain and even expand this scandalous anti-solidarity and anti-evangelization prejudice. More sadly, some of these Catholic institutional leaders even direct their business managers to pay large sums of money to outside 'consulting firms' in order *to prevent, to weaken, and even to destroy unions in Catholic institutions.*[3]

On the positive side, however, there remain a significant number of Catholic institutional leaders who continue to follow Catholic Social Teaching, and to witness to the truth of the dignity of all human persons by recognizing unions within their institutions, and by bargaining collectively with their fully human employees. Such leaders deserve our *grateful praise.*[4]

Materialist Philosophy
of Anti-Union Libertarian Economics

Among Catholic leaders who reject Catholic teaching about universal human dignity by fighting against unions, some justify their

---

[3] See Patrick J. Sullivan, U.S. CATHOLIC INSTITUTIONS AND LABOR UNIONS 1960-1980 (University of America Press, 1985).

[4] For a list of Catholic institutions whose leaders follow Catholic Social Teaching and agree to collective bargaining with their employees, see the Catholic Labor Network's Catholic Employer Project, founded and directed by Clayton Sinyai, at: *http://www.catholiclabor.org/CatholicEmployerProject.htm.*

anti-union prejudice by appealing to the *libertarian economic philosophy* of socially corrosive *competitive individualism*.

Of course, we are not fundamentally competitive individuals, but rather we are – as Catholic Social Teaching insists – *social beings* who are responsible for each other. Those who hold the false doctrine of competitive individualism reinforce the words of Cain (murder of his brother Abel), when he responded to the Lord's inquiry with the words "Am I my brother's keeper?"[5]

Some of these misguided Catholic leaders even accept the false teachings of the so-called 'Austrian school' of vicious libertarian economics. This school is known today especially through the writings of *Ludwig von Mises* (1881–1979) and *Friedrich von Hayek* (1899–1992).[6]

It was later further developed by Hayek's discipline, *Milton Friedman* (1912-2006) and his so-called 'Chicago school' of modern economic thought.

Still worse, and incredibly, some Catholic leaders even accept the even more vicious nihilist-libertarian teachings of the Russian atheist-materialist philosopher known as *Ayn Rand* (1904-1982).[7]

The ignorance and naiveté of such misguided Catholic leaders is partly understandable, because massive sums of money have been spent, and still are being spent, to spread propaganda in favor of

---

[5] GENESIS 4:9.

[6] For a theoretical and practical critique of the 'Austrian school' from the viewpoint of both practical business experience and Catholic Social Teaching, see Angus Sibley, THE "POISONED SPRING" OF ECONOMIC LIBERTARIANISM – MENGER, MISES, HAYEK, ROTHBARD: A CRITIQUE FROM CATHOLIC SOCIAL TEACHING OF THE 'AUSTRIAN SCHOOL' OF ECONOMICS (Pax Romana / Cmica-usa, 2011).

[7] Her original name was Alisa Zinov'yevna Rosenbaum

the false doctrines of the 'Austrian school' and of Ayn Rand. Yet, I presume, few of these misguided Catholic leaders realize that the 'Austrian school' of libertarian economics, and the nihilistic teachings of Rand, are both actually *anti-religious philosophies of selfish materialism.*

The 'Austrian school' is grounded cosmologically in the *atomistic-mechanist philosophy* of the classical Greek philosopher of individualistic materialism, *Epicurus* (341-270 BCE). The same is true of the wider modern libertarian economic ideology. Early Catholic Christian leaders rejected Epicurus' individualist, materialist, and anti-religious philosophy. So how can some contemporary Catholic leaders now embrace such anti-Christian doctrines?[8]

The vicious economic materialism of the more extreme atheist philosopher of individualistic selfishness, Ayn Rand, can be traced to a significant degree to the nihilist German philosopher, Friedrich Nietzsche (1844-1900). (There is non-nihilist 'benevolent' reading of Nietzsche, but I do not believe that account can be sustained.)

To cultivate a popular following, Rand partially used the medium of literary novels, along with her formally philosophical texts. Her most famous novels were THE FOUNTAINHEAD (1943) and ATLAS SHRUGGED (1947). Through her novels, Rand promoted the pure Laissez-Faire Capitalism which has been unquestionably condemned by Catholic Social Teaching.[9]

---

[8] For more on Epicureanism's materialist and anti-religious influence on the modern economic thought of both Capitalism and Socialism, see my forthcoming book, SOCIAL ANALYSIS II: READING THE SIGNS OF THE TIMES FOR SOCIETY AND CHURCH AT THE END OF THE MODERN WORLD (projected for 2012 from Pacem in Terris Press).

[9] Reportedly, a prominent contemporary Catholic Member of the Congress of the United States has several times declared himself a devoted follower of Ayn

At Rand's funeral, there was reportedly a six-foot floral arrangement in the shape of a U.S. dollar. Now, decades after her death, the Ayn Rand Institute and the Atlas Society reportedly still promote her extreme atheistic-materialist ideology of individualistic selfishness, including on university campuses.

Some Catholic Leaders Now Supporting Communist Repression of Labor

Within the pro-business and anti-labor imbalance of late modern bourgeois globalization, many U.S. Catholic business and political leaders have embraced – perhaps without realizing its destructive significance – yet another great deviation from Catholic Social Teaching, namely *a bizarre partnership with the repressive dictatorial communist government presently controlling China*. This is astounding since the Catholic Church has opposed Communism's repressive dictatorships, sometimes even at the price of martyrdom.

Since the last several decades of the 20th century, however, many Catholic leaders in business and politics have voiced no objections to, and some have even promoted, the closing of unionized industrial factories in the United States in order to export formerly U.S. unionized industrial jobs to a country controlled by Communism.

Yet, under the communist government of China, which, again, is a *political and economic dictatorship*, unjust violent state oppression abounds, workers have no truly free voice, and there are *no truly free democratic unions*.[10]

Rand yet, as we have seen, she was an atheistic-materialist philosopher of selfish individualism, Ayn Rand.

[10] China does have state-controlled unions, which simply follow the policies of China's Communist Party. Leaders of truly democratic unions elsewhere do

Thus, paradoxically, many U.S. Catholic business and political leaders appear to have rejected the very principle of papally-supported free democratic workers' unions. They appear instead have entered into a political-economic alliance with a totalitarian dictatorship which represses free democratic unions.

The motive seems to be that allying with a communist dictatorship (or alternately with a fascist one), which represses the human rights of workers, proves *more profitable* than cooperative partnership with the fully human persons who have organized themselves into free democratic unions.

New Intellectual Attempts to Play Down Catholic Social Teaching's Support of Workers' Unions

In addition, within this late modern global anti-labor bourgeois prejudice, some contemporary Catholic intellectuals are attempting to market *a false version of Catholic Social Teaching stripped of its century-long and still continuing prophetic support for workers' unions.*

This false version of Catholic Social Teaching is more subtle than blatant attacks on unions claiming that unions are evil. This alternative simply minimizes and then quietly *eliminates* Catholic Social Teaching's essential teaching about workers' unions.

Such intellectual 'sanitizing' of Catholic Social Teaching proclaims noble and spiritual messages about management and business

---

not consider China's unions to be free democratic workers' organizations. Dictators generally oppose free democratic unions. For example, among Adolf Hitler's first targets for elimination, reportedly as requested by many in the highest level of German business, were Germany's leaders of free democratic unions. At the time, many high-level U.S. business leaders, who reportedly helped to finance Hitler's rise to power, also reportedly supported Hitler's anti-union bias.

leadership. These messages are then presented repeatedly and at great length in conferences and publications as the 'spiritual' approach to management and business leadership. But, such conferences and publications normally never seem to mention Catholic Social Teaching in prophetic support for workers' unions.

These intellectuals teach the tradition as if this *essential* part of the Doctrine were not relevant to its 'spiritual' message for today's business leaders. They present the equivalent of what the great Lutheran theologian, Dietrich Bonhoeffer, called *cheap grace*.

By reducing Catholic Social Teaching to a 'spiritual' management theory which blocks out unions, these distortions subtly try to ideologize the Catholic tradition to conform to late modern Global Capitalism's *anti-union bourgeois class prejudice*. Again, the seductive power of this false teaching is not stated. Authentic Catholic teaching in support of workers' unions simply *vanishes*.

But workers' unions have not vanished, and they won't vanish – neither from Catholic teaching, nor from economic reality. Catholic Social Teaching's prophetic support for worker's unions remains, and will continue to remain, as will remain the desire of workers across the world to organize themselves into unions and to defend the unions they have already created.

Note the recent powerful words of Benedict XVI:

> *Through the combination of social and economic change, trade union organizations experience greater difficulty in carrying out their task of representing the interests of workers, partly because Governments, for reasons of economic utility, often limit the freedom or the negotiating capacity of labor unions. Hence traditional networks of solidarity have more and more obstacles to overcome.*

The repeated calls issued within the Church's social doctrine, beginning with Rerum Novarum [60], for the promotion of workers' associations that can defend their rights must therefore be honored today even more than in the past, as a prompt and far-sighted response to the urgent need for new forms of cooperation at the international level, as well as the local level.[11]

How important today, therefore, that Catholic episcopal, presbyteral, diaconal, religious, and lay leaders, in order

- to follow the call of the Holy Spirit,
- to remain faithful to their vocation as disciples of Jesus,
- to sustain evangelization of the working classes,

how important that these leaders begin to plan how Catholicism – in the United States and across the globe – might remain faithful to its teaching as a *prophetic institutional supporter of workers and their unions.*

(I will offer some recommendations for this possibility in my concluding reflections at the end of this book.)

How important, therefore, that all Catholic leaders study the *full truth* of Catholic Social Teaching, including its *essential pro-union teaching* as found in RERUM NOVARUM and in the four subsequent papal encyclicals, from 1931 to 1991, all of which commemorate, deepen, and celebrate its prophetic pro-union teaching.

---

[11] CARITAS IN VERITATE, Paragraph 25. The full text is available from the website of the Holy See at:
http://www.vatican.va/holy_father/benedict_xvi/encyclicals/documents/hf_ben-xvi_enc_20090629_caritas-in-veritate_en.html (accessed 2012-05-01).

Remembering the Five
Landmark Pro-Union Papal Encyclicals

To help to counter the growing *bourgeois alienation* of many Catholic leaders within the United States and elsewhere from the late modern industrial working classes, as well as the new *false teaching* that minimizes and even eliminates Catholic Social Teaching's support for workers unions, and in response to the growing *institutional breakdown* of Catholic evangelization within the late modern working classes, our Pax Romana federation has published this book.

This book makes clear the official 100 years of Catholic Social Teaching defending the rights and duties of both workers and employers, upholding their joint responsibility for work, and insisting on *the indispensible role of workers' unions* within industrial societies as a key mediating institution, as essential for human solidarity, and as requiring Catholic support from by the Church's strategy to evangelize the working classes.

This book pursues that goal by offering extended summaries of, and commentaries on, *the five great prophetic papal encyclicals written in prophetic defense of workers and their unions.* Four of these documents commemorate an anniversary of the first one. These five documents are:

1. RERUM NOVARUM, by Leo XIII, 1891

2. QUADRAGESIMO ANNO, by Pius XI, 1931

3. MATER ET MAGISTRA, by John XXIII, 1961

4. LABOREM EXERCENS, by John Paul II, 1981

5. CENTESIMUS ANNUS, by John Paul II, 1991

These five documents make clear the core commitment of contemporary Catholic Social Teaching to workers' natural and essential right to organize themselves into a union.[12]

Since, however, these documents are sometimes written in a style that may be difficult for some people to follow, this book hopefully provides a more easily understandable summary of each encyclical. It also intersperses each summary with commentaries which will hopefully make the documents more intelligible.

There are, of course, many other important papal social encyclicals which are not devoted in a major way to defense of workers' unions. Important as these other documents are for other purposes, they are not summarized here, since they do not focus in a major way on workers and workers' unions.

In that regard, the recent and moving 2009 social encyclical letter by Benedict XVI, CARITAS IN VERITATE, is not primarily devoted to the core theme of workers and their unions. That excellent encyclical is devoted to the equally important theme of "integral development." It builds on Paul VI's 1969 social encyclical POPULORUM PROGRESSIO, which addressed the same theme.

---

[12] Note that, while Pius XII (1939-1958) did not issue a papal encyclical to commemorate RERUM NOVARUM, he did on Pentecost of 1941 deliver an important radio message to mark its 50th Anniversary. But that address is not summarized here, since it did not have the same status as an encyclical. (John XXIII's 1961 commemorative encyclical, MATER ET MAGISTRA, includes a summary of that radio message.) Also Paul VI (1963-1978), while he did not issue an encyclical to commemorate the 80th anniversary of RERUM NOVARUM in 1971, did direct a public Apostolic Letter, titled OCTAGESIMA ADVENIENS, to Cardinal Maurice Roy, President of Council of the Laity and of the Pontifical Commission Justice and Peace. But, again, that letter is not included here since it did not have the status of an encyclical.

Nonetheless, since CARITAS IN VERITATE does include two important paragraphs on unions, those paragraphs have been added here in the Appendix at the end of this book. Plus the first of those (paragraph 25) has been quoted in this Introduction.

In conclusion, it may be helpful to point out that Catholic Social Teaching on workers and workers' unions inextricably flows from key social principles within this rich wisdom tradition. Among others, these principles include:

- The dignity of the human person
- The social nature of the human person
- The need for human solidarity
- The need for mediating institutions
- The preferential option for the poor

Thus, Catholic Social Teaching's support for workers and their unions within industrial societies, and for the right of workers to organize themselves into unions and to defend their unions from attack, is not something optional for Catholics. This teaching is deeply rooted in the above principles and has long been enshrined as a *core magisterial theme* of contemporary Catholic Social Teaching. Ultimately, it is rooted in the Gospel message of Jesus and the entire Biblical tradition. Not to understand this importance of this teaching is, sadly, not fully to understand Jesus' own message.

Let us now turn to the summaries of these five most important papal documents supporting workers and their unions.

2

RERUM NOVARUM

"On the Condition of the Working Class"
1891 Social Encyclical of Leo XIII

Developed from the original manuscript for Joe Holland's
MODERN CATHOLIC SOCIAL TEACHING
THE POPES CONFRONT THE INDUSTRIAL AGE 1740-1958
Paulist Press, 2003

Charter of Modern Social Catholicism

In 1891, Pope Leo XIII (1878-1903) published RERUM NOVARUM, widely seen as his greatest encyclical and often called the "Charter of Social Catholicism."[1]

The title means "of new things," but the encyclical has often been given the name, "On the Condition of the Working Class." "New things" refers, of course, to the Industrial Revolution. Leo was the first modern pope directly to address the Industrial Revolution, albeit, as noted, more than a century after it began and nearly half a century after Karl Marx and Friedrich Engels published their 1848 COMMUNIST MANIFESTO.

---

[1] The official English version of the text may on the website of the Vatican at: *http://www.vatican.va/holy_father/leo_xiii/encyclicals/documents/hf_l-xiii_enc_150518 91_rerum-novarum_en.html* (accessed 2012-05-01).

As also noted earlier, RERUM NOVARUM was too late for many of the Catholic areas of Western Europe, which had already industrialized during the *first stage* of Industrial Capitalism and suffered heavy Catholic losses. But it was not too late for the new immigrant working classes of the Industrial Capitalism's *second stage* in the English-speaking regions of the industrializing world.

By the time of RERUM NOVARUM, Catholic evangelization of the industrial working classes in the first region had already been crippled by pastoral failure. But the support for the Leonine pro-labor strategy by Catholic leadership in the English-speaking world led there to a flourishing evangelization of the working classes, especially within the German, Irish, Italian, and Slavic industrial diasporas.

If length of the text has any meaning, this encyclical was Leo's longest. Of his eighty-six encyclicals in Sr. Claudia Carlin's collection of English translations of the papal encyclicals, only nine exceed ten pages, with most running in the two-to-six-page range. Exceeding all is RERUM NOVARUM with *twenty-two* pages.[2]

RERUM NOVARUM came late in Leo's strategic design, long after an encyclical warning on Socialism, after another in defense of the family, after yet another attacking freemasonry, and after four major encyclicals on the Church and politics.

---

[2] Of Leo's longer documents, six in the Carlin collection range between eleven and fourteen pages (AETERNI PATRIS, ARCANUM, HUMANUM GENUS, IMMORTALE DEI, LIBERTAS, and SAPIENTIE CHRISTIANAE, all key strategic documents), while two later documents range between sixteen and twenty pages (PROVIDENTISSIMUS DEUS in 1893 on the study of the Bible, and SATIS COGNITUM in 1896 on the unity of the Church). See five volumes of the series, THE PAPAL ENCYCLICALS (Pierian Press, various dates).

Leo's four earlier letters on politics suggest that he had originally conceived his strategy as aimed primarily at political elites. But, as the machine revolution of Industrial Capitalism's second or national stage unfolded, and as the ranks of the industrial working class grew dramatically in the Catholic regions, Leo finally agreed to address the social question in a direct and substantial way.

Certainly, he was pressured by growing socialist competition for the loyalty of the expanding industrial working class, by the need for pastoral engagement with the new industrial working class in the local churches of the industrializing countries, and by his own turn to the laity for support against anti-Catholic elements behind the continental European form of the modern liberal state.

The text of Leo's RERUM NOVARUM may be divided into seven parts:

- Opening statement of the economic problem
- Critique of Socialism as a false remedy
- Correct remedy offered by the Church
- Role of the Church in this remedy
- Role of the State in this remedy
- Role of employers and workers in this remedy
- Concluding summary

The Economic Problem

In the first part as the opening statement of the problem, Leo noted that the spirit of revolutionary change had now "passed beyond the sphere of *politics* and made its influence felt in the cognate sphere of *economics*." (Italics added.)

Explaining why this had happened, Leo noted disturbing phenomena associated with the rise of Industrial Capitalism:

The elements of conflict now raging are unmistakable, in the vast expansion of industrial pursuits and the marvelous discoveries of Science; in the changed relations between masters and workmen; in the enormous fortunes of some few individuals, and the utter poverty of the masses; in the increased self-reliance and closer mutual combination of the working classes.[3]

But faithful to his spiritual-cultural analysis, Leo added a religious note by including "the prevailing moral degeneracy."[4]

In light of this urgent situation, just as in the past Leo had felt compelled to issue letters bearing on political matters, so now he declared: "We have thought it expedient to speak on the condition of the working classes." But he warned: "It is no easy matter to define the relative rights and mutual duties of the rich and of the poor, of capital and of labor." He further warned that "crafty agitators" were taking advantage of the situation "to stir up the people to revolt."[5]

A proximate cause of the social problem, Leo proposed, was that in the last century "the ancient workingmen's guilds were abolished, and no other protective organization took their place." Thus, just as laws set aside religion, so too

... by degrees it has come to pass that workingmen have been surrendered, isolated and helpless, to the hard-heartedness of employers and the greed of unchecked competition. The mischief has been increased by rapacious usury, which, although more than once condemned by the Church, is nevertheless, under a different

---

[3] Par. 1.

[4] Par. 1.

[5] Par. 2.

guise, but with like injustice, still practiced by covetous and grasping men. To his must be added that the hiring of labor and the conduct of trade are concentrated in the hands of comparatively few; so that a small number of very rich men have been able to lay upon the teeming masses of the laboring poor a yoke little better than slavery itself.[6]

Socialism as a False Remedy

In the second part of RERUM NOVARUM, Leo argued that the socialists had proposed a false remedy to the social question. "Working on the poor man's envy of the rich," they have striven "to do away with private property," so that all should become "common property" and be "administered by the State." But, Leo argued, this false solution was wrong because it would hurt the worker, the family, and the wider society.[7]

First, Leo claimed, in the socialist solution of state-administered community property, "the working man himself would be the first to suffer." For workers would not be able to invest savings in land, would lose "the workingman's little estate" and "the liberty of disposing of his wages, and thereby the hope and possibility of increasing his resources and of bettering his condition."[8]

Such a loss would be against justice, Leo argued, since the right to possess *property* was rooted in the fact that humans have reason, in contrast to other animals. The possession of reason gave humans the power of choice, he maintained, and the right to hold things in stable and permanent possession, because through reason humans

---

[6] Par. 3.

[7] Par. 4.

[8] Par. 5.

can link the future with the present and "lay provision for the future."

Leo then elaborated a traditional claim that labor's transformation of natural resources, so necessary to meet human needs and especially over the long term, gave a real title to property. To work the land and to transform it, and then to turn it over to someone else for ownership, would be unjust.

Leo further noted that this practice of private property had been consecrated by the tradition "of all ages," had been confirmed by civil laws derived from the natural law, and had been defended by divine sanction in Deuteronomy 5:21.[9]

In developing this argument about the right to private property, Leo made two interesting claims that went beyond the property issue.

On the one hand, in an *ecological* way he linked human property to nature and particularly to land, by saying that the supplies which humans need came from Earth and its fruit. Clearly Leo's normative model of labor was in direct relation to Earth. Even if a worker did not work directly with the land, he argued, at least his savings could enable the worker to purchase a "little estate" for permanently sharing the fruits of nature. On the other hand, he asserted that "Man precedes the State," and that, therefore, humans "possesses, prior to the State, the right of providing for substance."

On the other hand, in the face of the modern secular state's encroachment on religion, family, and even the individual, Leo also laid down the defensive principle that *the state is a secondary insti-*

---

[9] Pars. 6-7.

tution and must remain limited. His claim that "Man precedes the State" would become even more important with his successors, as both left-wing communist and right-wing fascist totalitarian states would push state encroachment to an absolute scope.[10]

Second, Leo argued that the socialist solution violated these same rights in a much stronger way in regard to the *family*. The family, he claimed, is "a true society, and one older than any State," and consequently "it has rights and duties peculiar to itself which are quite independent of the State."

The right of property was particularly important here, Leo argued, though he ascribed the right not to the family as a whole, but rather, following the classical patriarchal Roman model, to the *paterfamilias*. Only the "father ... in his capacity as head of the family" must "provide food and all necessities for those whom he has begotten." The father's personality, he then argued, was extended in his children, who carried on the right to his property.

While Leo's patriarchal model would prove problematic in the future, his claim that the family was "prior to the community" and has rights that were "founded more immediately in nature," would be another important resource against the looming horizon of totalitarianism. Leo concluded his section on family by again challenging the socialists, who, he stated, "in setting aside the parent and setting up a State supervision, act against natural justice, and destroy the structure of the home."[11]

Third, against the socialist remedy of state-administered community property, Leo made an argument frequently repeated later in

---

[10] Pars. 7-10.

[11] See par. 14 for this quote, and pars. 12-14 for his full discussion on family.

reference to Communism, namely that the whole civil society would be afflicted by a loss of motivation, and equality would become nothing more than "one dead level." Thus he prophesied:

> To how intolerable and hateful a slavery citizens would be subjected. The door would be thrown open to envy, to mutual invective, and to discord; the sources of wealth themselves would run dry, for no one would have any interest in exerting his talents of his industry; and that ideal equality about which they entertain pleasant dreams would be in reality the leveling down of all to a like condition of misery and degradation.[12]

Church's True Remedy

In the third part of RERUM NOVARUM, in contrast to the "false remedy" of the socialists, Leo offered what he proposed was the Church's true remedy.

"No practical solution of this question will be found," he declared, "apart from the intervention of religion and of the Church." And again, "It is we who are the chief guardian of religion." And once more, "all striving of men will be vain if they leave out the Church."[13]

To preface his proposal for a solution, Leo began by unfolding his philosophy of society. Against the modern *atomistic-mechanistic* idea of individual equality, he upheld what he claimed was nature's own celebration of "manifold differences" among people – "in capacity, skill, health, strength," with "unequal fortune" being "a necessary result of unequal condition." These natural dif-

---

12 Par. 15.

13 Par. 16.

ferences actually aided the whole community, for different people needed to play different parts in community life.[14]

Regarding "bodily labor," Leo argued that not work but only unhappiness in work was the result of sin. Yet to attempt to restructure society so as to eliminate all suffering in work would represent "lying promises" which would only "bring forth worse evils than the present."[15]

"The great mistake" in this deception, Leo claimed, was to assume that the social classes were naturally hostile, "that the wealthy and the working men are intended by nature to live in mutual conflict." He appealed to the premodern organic-hierarchical paradigm for society.

> Just as the symmetry of the human frame is the result of the suitable arrangement of the different parts of the body, so in a State it is ordained by nature that these two classes should dwell in harmony and agreement, so as to maintain the balance of the body politic.[16]

Then came Leo's clearest articulation of the foundational ethical principle for his solution: **"Each needs the other; capital cannot do without labor, nor labor without capital."**[17] (Bold added.) Here, he proposed, the Church could be of great aid.

> There is no intermediary more powerful than religion (whereof the Church is the interpreter and guardian) in drawing the rich

---

[14] Par. 17.

[15] Par. 18.

[16] Par. 19.

[17] Par. 19.

and the working class together, by reminding each of its duties to the other, and especially of the obligation of justice.[18]

Leo then spelled out the duties of justice on the one hand for "the proletarian and the worker" and on the other hand for "the wealthy owner and the employer." Since the recounting of these reciprocal duties is central to the encyclical, I will cite his words.

On one side the worker was obliged

> ... *to perform the work which has been freely and equitably agreed upon; never to injure the property, nor to outrage the person, of an employer; never to resort to violence in defending their own cause, nor to engage in riot or disorder; and to have nothing to do with men of evil principles, who work upon the people with artful promises of great result, and excite foolish hopes which usually end in useless regrets and grievous loss.*[19]

On the other side the employed was obliged

> ... *not to look upon their work people as their bondsmen, but to respect in every man in his dignity as a person ennobled by Christian character ... to see that the worker has time for his religious duties; that he be not exposed to corrupting influences and dangerous occasions; and that he not be led away to neglect his home and family, or to squander his earnings. Furthermore, the employer must never tax his work people beyond their strength, or employ them in work unsuited to their sex and age.*[20]

With special emphasis, Leo noted the employer's obligation to pay a just wage.

---

[18] Par. 19.

[19] Par. 20.

[20] Par. 20.

His great and principal duty is to give everyone what is just.
Doubtless, before deciding whether wages are fair, many things
have to be considered; but wealthy owners and all masters of labor
should be mindful of this – that to exercise pressure upon the in-
digent and the destitute for the sake of gain, and to gather one's
profit out of the need of another, is condemned by all laws, human
and divine. To defraud anyone of wages that are his due is a great
crime which cries to the avenging anger of Heaven.[21]

Finally, he elaborated on the just wage.

Lastly, the rich must religiously refrain from cutting down the
workmen's earnings, whether by force, by fraud, or by usurious
dealing; and with all the greater reason because the laboring man
is, as a rule, weak and unprotected, and because his slender means
should in proportion to their scantiness be accounted sacred.[22]

Along with his modern call for justice, Leo also held up the traditional perspective of charity which maintained that the rich would
be saved by munificent almsgiving. Regarding the rich, he harshly
warned that "riches do not bring freedom from sorrow and are of
no avail for eternal happiness, but rather are obstacles." He further
warned that "the rich should tremble at the threatening of Jesus
Christ."[23]

Then Leo repeated the "most excellent rule for the right use of
money," the rule which distinguished between the possession of
money and its use. He repeated the teaching of Aquinas that defended the right of private property, but insisted on its *social na-*

---

[21] Par. 20.

[22] Par. 20.

[23] Par. 22.

ture, namely that, after one's own needs (or one's family's needs) were met according to one's station in life, then the remainder must be given to the poor. Anyone who possessed "temporal blessings" was but "the steward of God's providence, for the benefit of others."[24]

Regarding the poor, Leo reminded his readers that "in God's sight poverty is no disgrace," and that workers should not be ashamed of "earning their bread by labor." For Christ, "whereas He was rich, for our sakes became poor," and "being the Son of God, and God Himself, chose to seem and to be considered the son of a carpenter."

Indeed, Leo said, he "did not disdain to spend a great part of His life as a carpenter Himself." Thus, "God Himself seems to incline rather to those who suffer misfortune" and "displays the tenderest charity toward the lowly and the oppressed."[25]

Such a perspective on riches and poverty, Leo maintained, would make the pride of the rich disappear and enable "rich and poor to join hands in friendly concord." The two classes would then be "not only united in the bonds of friendship, but also in those of brotherly love." They would understand that they had "the same common Father, who is God" and "the same common end, which is God himself."[26]

---

[24] Par. 22. This section on the obligations of the rich is the longest numbered paragraph in the document, with the one on the mutual obligations of justice between capital and labor being the second longest.

[25] Pars. 23-24.

[26] Pars. 24-25.

Role of the Church

In the fourth section of RERUM NOVARUM, Leo spelled out the role of the Church in applying this remedy. The Church's basic role, he maintained, was "to teach and to educate men," which it did through the intermediary of "her bishops and clergy."[27] This contribution of the Church was unique, because it alone "can reach the innermost heart and conscience, and bring men to act from a motive of duty, to control their passions and appetites, to love God and their fellow men with a love that is outstanding."[28]

Leo then noted how in the past "civil society was renovated in every part by Christian institutions." So too, "if human society is to be healed now, in no other way can it be healed save by a return to Christian life and Christian institutions." Only the Church, he claimed, could "restore" society to a path of class harmony.

This restoration would not be just spiritual, for the restoration of Christian morality would inevitably promote "temporal prosperity" in two ways, by restraining the greed for excessive possession and the thirst for pleasure.[29]

In addition, Leo pointed out, the Church "intervenes directly in behalf of the poor" though its many "associations which she knows to be efficient for the relief of poverty." This direct assistance to the poor goes back to beginning when Christians shared their goods with each other, to the ancient order of deacons, and to the subsequent patrimony of the Church, which has been "guarded with religious care as the inheritance of the poor."

---

[27] Par. 26.

[28] Par. 26.

[29] Pars. 27-28.

Role of the State

In the fifth part of RERUM NOVARUM Leo turned to the proper role of the state in the new context. This was an especially long part of the encyclical, no doubt because of Leo's great interest in politics. He articulated both a positive role for the state, in contrast to the negative understanding of Laissez-Faire Liberalism, and yet limited that role, in contrast to the expansive ambitions of modern liberal states.

It may be simplest to list his several points, with a brief comment on each.

- *Forms of Government.* First, Leo again made clear that he was not endorsing any particular form of government, and that any form of government was acceptable, provided it conformed to "right reason and natural law" and to the principles that he had laid out in his key encyclical on politics, IMMORTALE DEI.[30]

- *The Common Good.* Second, the fundamental task of the state, Leo maintained, was *"to serve the common good"* (italics added). In addition to the many functions associated with the modern state, he insisted that this also included "moral rule, well-regulated family life, (and) respect for religion and justice." Further, the more the state could do "for the benefit of the working class by the general laws of the country, the less need there will be so seek for special means to relieve them."[31]

- *Justice and Differences.* Third, Leo proposed, the commonwealth needed to be understood in an organic manner with all classes, and especially the working class that formed the major-

---

[30] Par. 32.

[31] Par. 32.

ity, making up real parts of its body. In this organic context, "the first and chief" duty of rulers "is to act with strict justice – with that justice which is called *distributive* – toward each and every class alike."

Leo further noted that it was "only by the labor of working men that States grow rich," and therefore the state must especially watch over the interests of the working class. But he also argued that there were natural "differences and inequalities" in the citizenry, which were then expressed as class differences, no matter what the form of government, and that the state needs to respect these inequalities.

(This is why the Catholic Social Teaching, tracing its roots back to Aristotle, has argued that distributive justice is guided by an equity proportionate to the station-in-life of the various classes.[32])

- *A Limited State.* Fifth, Leo also argued for a limited state. Thus he wrote, "The state must not absorb the individual or the family." In this regard, he noted, the object of the government of the state should not be "the advantage of the ruler," but "the

---

[32] Pars. 33-34. Following Aristotle, scholastic philosophy had distinguished distributive and commutative justice. *Distributive justice* serves the common good through the legal guidance of the distribution of resources according to a principle of proportionate equality. Thus, the state was to guarantee that the organic role of the working class, both in the workplace and in wages, be defended through legislation which protects its proportionate right as an authentic part of the social whole, and do this in the name of the common good. Later a new phrase would be introduced to guide reflection on justice for labor, namely the concept of *social justice*, but this concept was not yet present in Leo's thought. See Johannes Messner, SOCIAL ETHICS: NATURAL LAW IN THE WESTERN WORLD, trans. J.H. Doherty (St. Louis: B. Herder Book, 1965), pp. 319-324.

benefit of those over whom the ruler is placed." For the ruler's power to rule came from God, as a participation in divine sovereignty, and so needed to be exercised with the same "fatherly solicitude" by which God guided both the community as a whole and each individual in it.[33]

Leo offered extensive comments on how "the public authority" needed to intervene or "to step in," whenever "the general interest or any particular class suffers, or was threatened with harm," provided that need could not be met in another way. The areas of state-intervention that Leo mentioned included religious observance and family life, moral standards, justice, the development of youth, and military service.

In particular, Leo saw "a strike of workers" as an occasion for state intervention, if there were "imminent danger of disturbance to the public peace," as well as "danger to morals through the mixing of the sexes," and workplace dangers to health. In such cases, "it would be right to invoke the aid and authority of the law," though "the law must not undertake more, nor proceed further, than was required for the remedy of the evil."[34]

Also, Leo argued, the state had the obligation to protect rights, and especially the rights of the poor.

> *The poor and badly off have a claim to especial consideration. The richer class have many ways of shielding themselves, and stand less in need of help from the State; whereas the mass of the poor have no resources of their own to fall back upon, and must chiefly depend upon the assistance of the State. And it is for this reason*

---

[33] Par. 35.

[34] Par. 36.

that wage-earners, since they mostly belong in the mass of the needy, should be specially cared for and protected by the government.[35]

At the same time, Leo stressed the duty of the state "of safeguarding private property." Here he warned of the danger of socialist revolution.

Most true it is that by far the larger part of the workers prefers to better themselves by honest labor rather than by doing any wrong to others. But there are not a few who are imbued with evil principles and eager for revolutionary change, whose main purpose is to stir up disorder and incite their fellows to acts of violence. The authority of the law should intervene to put restraint upon such firebrands, to save the working classes from being led astray by their maneuvers, and to protect lawful owners from spoliation.[36]

Yet Leo recognized that workers sometimes resort to strikes for just reasons, but he urged the state to prevent strikes by eliminating the conditions that generate them.

When working people have recourse to a strike and become voluntarily idle, it is frequently because the hours of labor are too long, or the work too hard, or because they consider their wages insufficient ... the laws should forestall and prevent such troubles from arising; they should lend their influence and authority to the removal in good time of the causes which lead to conflicts between employers and employed.[37]

---

[35] Par. 37.

[36] Par. 38.

[37] Par. 39.

Then Leo offered several long paragraphs on the duty of the state to protect the "interests" of the worker, particularly "the interests of his soul," since the worker "is made after the image and likeness of God." The pope stressed the transcendence of human dignity over all the rest of creation, and condemned anything that would diminish the dignity of the worker. He then added the state's duty to protect "the obligation of the cessation from work on Sundays and certain holy days."

He urged the state "to save unfortunate working people from the cruelty of the greedy, who use human beings as mere instruments for money-making" through "excessive labor," and even employ children and women in workshops and factories. Regarding children, Leo noted, they should not be allowed to work in these places "until their bodies and minds are sufficiently developed." Regarding women, he argued in a traditionalist manner that they "are not suited for certain occupations," and that "a woman is by nature fitted for home-work."[38]

Leo rejected the liberal economic teaching that wages, "as we are told, are regulated by free consent." This leaves out, he insisted, several "important considerations," namely that labor is both personal and necessary. In a direct challenge to the Laissez-Faire liberal teaching, he held up what would later be called the principle of the "living wage." "There underlies a dictate of justice more imperious and ancient than any bargain between man and man, namely, that wages ought not to be insufficient to support a frugal and well-behaved wage-earner." Such a living wage could be de-

---

[38] Pars. 40-42.

termined, he said, by appropriate societal boards, with the state providing "sanction and protection" for their decisions.[39]

Apparently without canonizing the added notion of a "family-wage" (the question would remain unsettled in Catholic Social Teaching well after RERUM NOVARUM), he noted that, if a worker's wage were sufficient to "comfortably support himself, his wife, and his children," the worker would be able to save, and could thereby procure a modest income, apparently from a small farm that "would add to the produce of the earth and to the wealth of the community."

He encouraged working people to obtain "a share in the land," both in order bridge the gap between rich and poor, and because "men always work harder and more readily ... on what belongs to them," as well as to avoid the perils of immigration. (Leo was especially concerned about the spiritual fate of Italians migrating to America, where they faced Protestant missionary campaigns.)[40]

Role of Employers and Employees

In the sixth part of RERUM NOVARUM, Leo addressed the role of "employers and workmen ... of themselves," that is, independently of Church and state.[41] Here he wrote first of "associations ...

---

[39] Pars. 43-45.

[40] Pars. 46-47. For Leo's concern about the Italian immigration to America, see his 1888 encyclical, QUAM AERUMNOSA in Carlin, PAPAL ENCYCLICALS, Vol. 2., pp. 191-194.

[41] Note that here Leo was reflecting the growing sense of a civil society apart from the state. Liberalism had, of course, defined civil society as separate and "private," in contrast to the traditionally "public" sphere of politics. Catholic social thought later did begin to accept the distinctive nature of this sphere of

which drew the two classes together," presumably the paternalistic clubs of employers and workers long developed in France. The task of these organizations, he said, was "mutual help. He also mentioned "benevolent foundations" established to help workers, their widows, or their orphans, in cases of calamity.[42]

Then comes the most dramatic section of the encyclical, its legitimization of *employees' unions*. At the start of Industrial Capitalism's second or national stage, many still looked upon unions as subversive. So for the pope to support them was astounding.

> *The most important of all these are workingmen's unions, for these virtually include all the rest. History attests what excellent results were brought about by the artificers' guilds of olden times. They were the means of affording not only many advantages to the workmen, but in no small degree of promoting the advancement of art, as numerous monuments remain to bear witness.*
>
> *These unions should be suited to the requirements of our age – an age of wider education, of different habits, and of far more numerous requirements in daily life. It is gratifying to know that there are actually in existence not a few associations of this nature, consisting either of workmen alone, or of workmen and employers together, but it were greatly to be desired that they should become more numerous and more efficient.[43]* (Bold added.)

---

common life, and for it developed the institutional category of "social justice." See Messner, SOCIAL ETHICS, pp. 323-224.

[42] Par. 48.

[43] Par. 49.

While Leo argued that unions were needed because of the weakness of individual workers in defending themselves, he also argued that unions were *a natural form of human community*. He stated that they existed "of their own right," that is, even apart from the need to defend the workers against exploitation from ruthless employers.

> *It is this natural impulse which binds men together in civil society; and it is likewise this which leads them to join together in associations which are, it is true, lesser and not independent societies, but, nevertheless, real societies.*[44]

Further, he argued, societies like unions, which are formed within "the bosom of the commonwealth," even though they are called "private," are nonetheless *part of the commonwealth* and as such cannot be prohibited by public authority.

> *For, to enter into a "society" of this kind is the natural right of man; and the State has for its office to protect natural rights, not to destroy them; and, if it forbids its citizens to form associations, it contradicts the very principle of its own existence, for both they and it exist in virtue of the like principle, namely, the natural tendency of man to dwell in society.*[45]

Here he compared these unions with the various "confraternities, societies, and religious orders" that arose in times past within the Church. In those times, Leo noted, rulers of state had tried to repress or control these organizations, but the Church had defended

---

[44] Par. 50.

[45] Par. 51.

their autonomy from the state, and their resulting freedom had brought many benefits to society.[46]

On the negative side, Leo warned that many associations of workers are "in the hands of secret leaders, and are managed on principles ill-according with Christianity and the public well-being." He argued that Christian workers should not join "associations in which their religion will be exposed to peril," but rather should "form associations among themselves and unite their forces so as to shake off courageously the yoke of so unrighteous and intolerable an oppression."[47] To fight socialist unions, Leo implicitly encouraged Christian unions. He also encouraged various discussion groups, made up of "men of eminence," to promote practical action on behalf of workers.[48]

Final Summary

The sixth and final section of RERUM NOVARUM was Leo's summary. Here he emphasized again workers' associations and the three themes of body, soul, and property, with particular emphasis on the religious foundation of these associations and the need to re-establish Christian morals. Thus, Leo ended his most important encyclical and the foundational one for the economic dimension of contemporary Catholic Social Teaching.[49]

---

[46] Par. 53.

[47] Par. 54.

[48] Pars. 54-55.

[49] Pars. 57-64.

3

QUADRAGESIMO ANNO

"On Reconstruction of the Social Order"
1931 Social Encyclical of Pius XI
Written for the 30ᵗʰ Anniversary of Rerum Novarum

Developed from the original manuscript for Joe Holland's
MODERN CATHOLIC SOCIAL TEACHING
THE POPES CONFRONT THE INDUSTRIAL AGE 1740-1958
Paulist Press, 2003

New Theme of Social Justice

I n 1931, Pius XI (1922-1939) published his famous commemorative encyclical, QUADRAGESIMO ANNO (meaning "in the for-
tieth year"), generally named in English *"On Reconstruction of the
Social Order."* It offered a 40ᵗʰ anniversary reflection on Leo XIII's
1891 foundational social encyclical, RERUM NOVARUM. It also up-
dated that document in light of new political-economic developments. In the list of key economic documents of Catholic Social
Teaching, this one stands second in line after RERUM NOVARUM.[1]

---

[1] The official English version may be found on the website of the Vatican at:
http://www.vatican.va/holy_father/pius_xi/encyclicals/documents/hf_p-
xi_enc_19310515_quadragesimo-anno_en.html (accessed 2012-05-01).

The encyclical is divided into three main parts, plus the Introduction and Conclusion. Thus, its structure is:

- Introduction
- Review of the benefits of RERUM NOVARUM
- Defense and development of the Church's social teaching
- Analysis of the root of the social problem and its remedy in Christian moral reform
- Conclusion

Introduction

Pius XI set the stage by recalling the modern industrial capitalist division of labor into two social classes, and he did so in terms even more sympathetic to workers than Leo XIII's original document.

> *From toward the close of the nineteenth century, the new kind of economic life that had arisen and the new developments of industry had gone to the point in most countries that human society was becoming divided more and more into two classes. One class, very small in number, was enjoying almost all the advantages which modern inventions so abundantly provided; the other, embracing the huge multitude of working people, oppressed by wretched poverty, was vainly seeking escape from the straits wherein it stood.*[2]

Immediately in this introduction, Pius XI rejected Socialism. But more sharply than Leo XIII, even while appealing to him, he did not call for a reform of Liberalism (meaning Capitalism in its initial Laissez Faire form), but identified Liberalism as a parallel danger.

---

[2] Par. 3.

(Leo) sought no help from either Liberalism or Socialism, for the one had proved that it was utterly unable to solve the social problem, and the other, proposing a remedy far worse than the evil itself, would have plunged human society into greater dangers.[3]

Again in his Introduction, Pius described Leo as having "boldly attacked and overturned the idols of Liberalism," and instead as having proclaimed a "new social philosophy," rooted in "the treasury of right reason and Divine Revelation."[4]

Part I.
Benefits of Rerum Novarum

In describing the benefits of Leo XIII's social encyclical, Pius identified three areas that had been helped: 1) the Church; 2) the State; and 3) the production system of employer and workers.

The Church

Pius claimed that the encyclical had aided the popes in their "defense especially of the poor and the weak," and that thanks to the document "scholars, both priests and laymen," had developed "a social and economic Science in accord with the conditions of our times." He commended "courses instituted at Catholic universities, colleges and seminaries," as well as "social congresses and (social-study) weeks."

As a result, he boasted, "Catholic principles on the social question have ... passed into the patrimony of all human society," such that "after the terrible war," the "leading nations" attempted to "re-

---

[3] Par. 10.

[4] Pars. 11 & 14.

store peace on the basis of a thorough reform of social conditions, (based on) the norms agreed upon to regulate in accordance with justice and equity the labor of workers." The pope also argued that Leo's teachings had been "widely diffused," that the "souls of workers" had been filled with "the Christian spirit," and that "new organizations" of "workers, draftsmen, farmers, and employees of every kind" had been founded "frequently under the leadership of priests."[5]

The State

Pius XI then proposed that Leo's teaching had helped governments move beyond "the confines imposed by Liberalism." Describing the liberal philosophy of government in negative laissez-faire terms as seeking only legal order, he described Leo as showing how the state needs positively through its laws to promote the common good.

In that process, he added, "chief consideration ought to be given to the weak and the poor." Describing "the principles of Liberalism as tottering," he added that "good Catholics" had been "champions of social legislation" in their legislatures.

Finally, he rejoiced that "a new branch of law" had emerged "to protect vigorously the sacred rights of workers," including

> ... the protection of life, health, strength, family, homes, workshops, wages and labor hazards, in fine, everything which pertains to the condition of wage workers, with special concern for women and children.[6]

---

[5] Pars. 17-24.

[6] Pars. 25-28.

Employers and Workers

Pius XI next celebrated the creation of "associations that embrace either workers alone (unions) or workers and employers together." He recalled the hostility that formerly was directed to "workers' associations" by "those at the helm of State, plainly imbued with Liberalism."[7] Such political leaders, he highlighted,

> ... *were showing little favor to workers' associations of this type; nay, rather they were going out of their way to recognize similar organizations of other classes and show favor to them, they were* **with criminal injustice denying the natural right to form associations** *to those who needed it most to defend themselves from ill treatment at the hands of the powerful.*[8] (Bold added.)

Leo's encyclical, the pope continued, "encouraged Christian workers to found mutual associations according to their various occupations." Such endeavors, he added, also protected them from "socialist organizations," which claimed "to be the sole defenders and champions of the lowly and oppressed." Such associations were to be "founded upon religion," so as to increase "the goods of body, of soul, and of property."[9]

---

[7] Pars. 29-30. Thus, Catholic Social Teachings supports both kinds of associations, one of workers alone to bargain with employers, and the other of workers and employers together. It is up to the workers themselves to choose which they prefer, but in both cases Catholic Social Teaching sees workers and employers ideally working together in a framework of justice.

[8] Par. 30.

[9] As a result of RERUM NOVARUM and QUADRAGESIMO ANNO there grew up a global network of Catholic-inspired 'Christian-Democratic' unions (eventually known as the *World Confederation of Labor* [WCL]), which flourished along with a larger secular democratic-socialist global network of unions (eventually known as the *International Confederation of Free Trade Unions* [ICFTU]) and also

In certain situations, however, he acknowledged that workers were "almost forced" to join "secular labor unions," but this was permissible provided they truly professed "justice and equity and (gave) Catholic members full freedom to care for their own conscience and obey the laws of the Church." In such situations, he declared:

> Side by side with these (secular) unions there should always be associations zealously engaged in imbuing and forming their members in the teaching of religion and morality so that they in turn may be able to permeate the unions with that good spirit.[10]

Pius XI expressed his regret that the spirit of forming Christian unions was not matched by zeal for employers to form their own Christian associations. He developed this theme of employers associations no further, apparently because there was little to praise.[11]

The pope concluded Part I of his document by naming Leo XIII's RERUM NOVARUM "the *Magna Charta* upon which all Christian activity in the social field ought to be based, as on a foundation."

---

a Soviet-controlled communist global network of unions (eventually known as the *World Federation of Trade Unions* [WFTU].

During the Cold War, these three global union networks engaged in strong competition. Curiously, the Christian-Democratic global union network came to include a vast number of Buddhist and Muslim members in Africa and Asia, who did not wish to be identified with either side of the Cold War, and the organization later re-defined itself as broadly spiritual rather than exclusively Catholic. After the fall of the Soviet Union, the communist WFTU declined but still survives. In 2006, the Christian-Democratic WCL merged with the secular democratic-socialist ICFTU to form the *International Trade Union Confederation* (ITUC).

[10] Par. 35 for the quotation, and pars. 31-35 for the preceding paragraph.

[11] Par. 38. Later, such organizations would in fact be developed.

Acknowledging, however, that both doubts as to "the correct meaning of some parts of Leo's Encyclical" and certain "controversies" that have arisen in regard to it, the pope then turned to a defense of the Church's authority to teach in the social arena.[12]

Part II.
Defense of Church Social Teaching

Pius XI began by defending the authority of the Church to teach in socio-economic matters. The laws of economics, he argued, are "based on the very nature of material things," and God is "the author of nature. Therefore, he continued, economics needs to be placed in its "proper place in the universal order of purposes," so that it may be oriented to "the final end of all things, that is, God."[13]

Right of Property

The first theme that Pius XI addressed in his defense of Church teaching was "ownership, or the right of property."

Following Aquinas, he argued that property had *both an individual and a social character*. When both were honored, he stated, society avoided the "twin shipwrecks" of "individualism" and "collectivism," which were promoted by the two wings of "social modernism" (Liberalism and Socialism). Because of property's dual character, he argued, "the right of property is distinct from its use." It is the task of "public authority" to define in details the duties of its use on behalf of "the common good.

---

12 Pars. 39-40.

13 Pars. 412-43.

Capital and Labor

While historically unclaimed property may be acquired by occupancy or labor, Pius noted, "work that is hired out" does not entitle one to ownership of that which is worked. Nonetheless, he continued, the claim of "Manchesterian Liberals" that the labor-contract is to be determined only by the free market is false. Because of this false claim, "capital has too long been able to appropriate too much to itself ... hardly leaving to the worker enough to restore and renew his strength."

On the contrary, as Leo XIII stated, "**Neither capital can do without labor, nor labor without capital**" (bold added). Again, the pope cited Leo's words, "However the earth may be apportioned among private owners, it does not cease to serve the common interests of all."

Then, adding in his own words a new phrase to the terminology of justice, he proclaimed, "By this law of *social justice*, one class is forbidden to exclude the other class from sharing in the benefits" (italics added).[14]

> To each, therefore, must be given his share of goods, and the distribution of created goods, which, as every discerning person knows, is laboring today under the gravest evils due to the huge disparity between the few exceedingly rich and the unnumbered propertyless, must be effectively called back to and brought into conformity with the norms of the common good, that is, "**social justice**"(bold added).[15]

---

[14] Par. 52-57.

[15] Par. 58.

The Propertyless, especially in Asia

Next, Pius XI lamented that "in our age of 'industrialism'" so many workers were without ownership, and especially in Asia:

> *Since manufacturing and industry have so rapidly pervaded and occupied countless regions not only in the countries called new, but also in the realms of the Far East that have been civilized from antiquity, the number of the non-owning poor has increased enormously and their groans cry to God from the earth.*
>
> *Added to them is the huge army of rural wage workers, pushed to the lowest level of existence and deprived of all hope of ever acquiring "some property in land," and, therefore, permanently bound to the status of non-owning worker unless suitable and effective remedies are applied.*
>
> *... the immense multitude of the non-owning workers on the one hand and the enormous riches of certain very wealthy men on the other establish an unanswerable argument that the riches which are so abundantly produced in our age of "industrialism," as it is called, are not rightly distributed and equitably made available to the various classes of the people.* [16]

The pope warned that, unless there were a rapid and socially just distribution of property, "let no one persuade himself that public order, peace, and the tranquility of human society can be effectively defended against the agitators of revolutions." [17]

---

[16] Pars. 59-60.

[17] Par. 61. With Pius' warning about the brutality of unregulated Liberal Capitalism unheeded, the Chinese Communist Revolution would finally triumph in 1949.

While defending the hiring contract as not unjust of itself, Pius nonetheless demanded that the pay be *just*. To determine what was just, he argued, required addressing three factors, plus one recommended enhancement.[18]

- *Family Wage.* First, "the worker must be paid a wage sufficient to support him and his family." Speaking from a traditional perspective, he argued that mothers "should work primarily in the home or in its immediate vicinity."

  He decried as "an intolerable abuse, and so to be abolished at all cost, for mothers on account of the father's low wage to be forced to engage of gainful occupations outside the home to the neglect of their proper cares and duties, especially the training of children."

  Here, Pius XI resolved in affirmative fashion the long debate following Rerum Novarum about whether or not Catholic Social Teaching supported a family wage.

- *Condition of Business.* Second, the pope also acknowledged that, in determining wage levels, it would be unjust to raise wages to a level that would destroy a business. But it would be wrong, he insisted, to underpay workers in order to sell a product at less than a just price.

- *Public Economic Good.* Third, workers' pay, he argued, needs to be set not so low as to increase unemployment. Opportunity to work, he continued, needs to be provided for all those who are willing to work.

---

[18] Pars. 63 & 74 for this and the following paragraphs on just pay.

Further, its level should be sufficient to allow the worker eventually "to attain gradually to the possession of a moderate amount of wealth." There should be "a right proportion among wages and salaries" that is "closely connected (with) a right proportion in the prices at which goods are sold by the various occupations."

- *Workers' Participation.* Finally, in an enhancement to Catholic Social Teaching, the pope considered it advisable that "the work-contract be somewhat supplemented by a partnership-contract" (sharing in ownership and/or management). In this way, he argued, "Workers and other employees thus become sharers in ownership or management, or participate in some fashion in the profits received."

Reconstruction of the Social Order

Pius XI next turned to the social order itself, which he said was greater than the preceding questions yet strongly influenced them. Two things were necessary, he claimed: 1) *reform of institutions*; and 2) *correction of morals.* Under these two headings, the pope offered three lengthy descriptions of institutional reforms, and a brief statement on moral reform.

- *Subsidiarity.* The pope's first concern under institutions was with the state. Here he worried that "individualism" had eroded the "rich social life which was once highly developed through associations of various kinds." What was left, he lamented, was only the naked relationship of individuals and the state, with the state forced to take over "all the burdens which the wrecked associations once bore.

In response, the pope offered his now famous and anti-totalitarian principle of *subsidiarity*.[19] So important is this principle in the Catholic social tradition that it may be helpful to cite the pope's full words.

> *Just as it is gravely wrong to take from individuals what they can accomplish by their own initiative and industry and give it to the community, so also it is an injustice and at the same time a grave evil and disturbance of right order to assign to a greater and higher association what lesser and subordinate organizations can do.*
>
> *For every social activity ought of its very nature to furnish help to the members of the body social, and never destroy and absorb them.*
>
> *The supreme authority of the State ought, therefore, to let subordinate groups handle matters and concerns of lesser importance, which would otherwise dissipate its efforts greatly. Thereby the State will more freely, powerfully, and effectively do all those things that belong to it alone because it alone can do them: directing, watching, urging, restraining, as occasion requires and necessity demands.*
>
> *Therefore, those in power should be sure that the more perfectly a graduated order is kept among the various associations, in observance of the principle of "subsidiary function," the stronger social authority and effectiveness will be the happier and more prosperous the condition of the State.*[20]

---

[19] Par. 78.

[20] Pars. 79-80.

- *Industries & Professions.* In what would later be a controversial and unclear teaching of this encyclical, Pius XI then called for associations between the individual and the state to be established in the economic arena. He likened these to the earlier guilds, which had organized workers into functional associations.

  Such economic associations were not to operate simply on the principle of competition, found in the free market, but rather from a "harmonious" arrangement of their social functions. The associations were to pursue the interests of their whole area of work, and to do so freely.[21]

- *Directing Authority.* Pius XI also warned that "the right ordering of economic life cannot be left to a free competition of forces" (something that he called "this evil individualistic spirit"). Rather it was necessary that "economic life be again subjected to and governed by a true and effective directing principle."

  Such a "directing principle" would be quite different from "economic dictatorship." There was needed "a juridical and social order which will, as it were, give form and shape to all economic life." This principle needs also to be expanded, he argued, to the level of nations through international treaties.

  Such an authority, described in the document as "a system of syndicates and corporations," would have the following characteristics.

  1) It would give "monopoly privilege" to "free syndicates" of workers or employers to make binding labor agreements.

---

[21] Pars. 81-87.

2) Delegates from workers and employers syndicates would form governing "corporations" for their industry, with strikes and lockouts forbidden, and with appeal to a higher governing "magistracy."

3) All would be governed by "Catholic principles." [22]

- *Reform of Morality.* Here Pius XI actually said little about the reform of morals, except to appeal to "right reason," and to warm against the danger of Socialism arising from the failure of the current economic system.

The precise nature of Pius XI's *corporativist* vision remains to this day unclear in Catholic Social Teaching. Further, the vision became tragically obscured by the authoritarian and brutal reality of Fascism which has also been described as corporativist.

Next the pope turned to the great changes that, he claimed, had developed in "the economic system (Liberal Capitalism) and Socialism ... since Leo XIII's time."

Part III.
Root Causes of the Social Crisis and its Remedy

Pius XI began this third section by offering his analysis of historical changes since Leo's time in terms of three themes: 1) Liberal Capitalism; 2) Socialism; and 3) "the Christian reform of morals."

However, the pope did not emphasize the word "Capitalism," but usually wrote non-ideologically of "this economic system" or "the contemporary economic regime." The word "capitalist" or "capitalistic" appeared only three times in the document, and all within a

---

[22] Pars. 88-96.

limited section (pars. 103, 104, & 112), while the words "socialist," "Socialism," "communist," or "Communism" appeared fifty-seven times. His preferred name for Capitalism was "Liberalism."

Nonetheless, this document represents, I believe, the first papal use of an explicit reference to Capitalism. In that regard, only in the twentieth century did 'Capitalism' become a common name even in secular discourse. The earlier name was typically the 'Liberal Political Economy, or in abbreviated form "Liberalism."

Changes in Capitalism

Pius XI began by appealing to Leo XIII to declare that "this economic system" was not itself unjust, but needed to be reformed.

> With all his energy Leo XIII sought to adjust (reform) this economic system according to the norms of right order; hence, it is evident that this system is not to be condemned it itself. And surely it is not of its own nature vicious. But it does violate right order when capital hires workers, that is, the non-owning working class, with a view to and under such terms that it directs business and even the whole economic system according to its own will and advantage, scorning the human dignity of the workers, the social character of economic activity and social justice itself, and the common good.[23]

The pope then noted that the "capitalist" economic regime was not the only alternative, and pointed to "agriculture, wherein the greater portion of mankind honorably and honestly procures its livelihood," although it too is "crushed with hardships and difficulties." Nonetheless, he continued, with "the diffusion of modern

---

[23] Par. 101.

industry throughout the world, the "capitalist" economic regime has spread everywhere."

Hence, in addressing this economic regime, Pius XI made clear – in a foretaste of the explicitly global strategy that began with John XXIII – that he was not speaking simply to the old industrial regions, but to "all mankind."[24]

The pope then addressed the changes in the "capitalist" regime since the time of Leo XIII. "

In the first place," he pointed to the management revolution and what he called an *"economic dictatorship"* (italics added). Since this is a classic statement of this pope, it may be helpful to cite the full text.

> *It is obvious that not only is wealth concentrated in our times but an immense power and **despotic economic dictatorship** is consolidated in the hands of a few, who often are not owners but only the trustees and managing directors of invested funds which they administer according to their own arbitrary will and pleasure (bold added).*

> *This dictatorship is being most forcibly exercised by those who, since they hold the money and completely control it, control credit also and rule the lending of money. Hence they regulate, so to speak, the life-blood whereby the entire economic system lives, and have so firmly in their grasp the soul, as it were, of economic life that no one can breathe against their will.[25]*

The cause of this "economic dictatorship," the pope claimed, was the "**unlimited freedom of struggle among competitors** ... which

---

[24] Pars. 102-103.

[25] Pars. 105-106.

lets only the strongest survive" (bold added). As a result, he continued, "this is the same as saying those who fight the most violently, those who give least heed to conscience."[26] The resulting "accumulation of might and of power," he then argued, "generates three kinds of conflict:"

- *The struggle for economic supremacy itself*
- *The bitter fight to gain supremacy over the State to use its resources and authority*
- *The conflict between States themselves* [27]

In the pope's analysis, the ultimate result is the paradoxical destruction of the free market by unbridled competition, and the degradation of the state into an instrument for greed. (Pius XI's criticism of Liberal Capitalism before the regulatory reforms of the mid-20th century reminds us of the destruction of regulatory reforms in the unregulated Global Capitalism which began in the late 20th century.)

In addition, he stated, the destructive pattern expands to the international level in two forms:

- *Economic nationalism or even economic imperialism*
- *And the no less deadly and accursed internationalism of finance or international imperialism, whose country is where profit is* [28]

Pope Pius XI's remedy was to be found, of course, in "Christian social philosophy," which he wrote "avoids the reefs of individualism and collectivism." The competitive freedom of the mar-

---

[26] Par. 107.

[27] Par. 108.

[28] Par. 109.

ket, he proposed, needs to be "brought under public authority" and there guided by "the norm of *social justice*" (italics added).[29]

Changes in Socialism

This encyclical also contained a landmark analysis of Socialism, in which for the first time a modern pope reflected upon the strategic split in the movement of the left. In the time of Leo XII, the pope noted, the two sections of Socialism (one dictatorial and revolutionary, and the other democratic and gradualist) were not radically separate, but in his time they had often become "bitterly hostile" to each other.

On one side, the pope described dictatorial and revolutionary "Communism" as the result of changes within the socialist movement, paralleling similar changes "within the capitalist economic system." Presumably, he meant that just as the nationalist stage of Capitalism had produced what he called a *nationalist economic dictatorship,* so the nationalist stage of Socialism had produced a *nationalist political dictatorship.*

Pius XI virulently condemned this dictatorial communist side of the split. Communism, he lamented, had inflicted "horrible slaughter and destruction" upon "vast regions of eastern Europe and Asia, sought unrelenting class warfare and absolute extermination of private property," and remained "openly hostile to Holy Church and to God himself."[30]

The other stream, he noted, "kept the name Socialism," but had become more moderate by rejecting violence, modifying the class

---

[29] Par. 110

[30] Par. 112.

struggle and the attack on private property, and even "in a certain measure approaching the reforming vision of Catholic Social Teaching.[31]

> *Socialism inclines toward and in a certain way approaches the truths which Christian tradition has always held sacred; for it cannot be denied that its demands at times come very near those that Christian reformers of society justly insist upon.[32]*

But, in face of the question of whether Christians and socialists might meet in some middle ground, and acknowledging that many Catholics were asking this question, he responded negatively that it was "a vain hope!" Rejecting any compromise or coalition, he declared:

> *We make this pronouncement: Whether considered as a doctrine, or an historical fact, or a movement, Socialism, if it remains truly Socialism, even after it has yielded to truth and justice on the points which we have mentioned, cannot be reconciled with the teachings of the Catholic Church because its concept of society itself is utterly foreign to Catholic truth.[33]*

For the pope, the reason that Socialism remained "utterly foreign" was that it ignored "the sublime end of both man and society," and affirmed that "human association has been instituted for the sake of material advantage alone. In this perspective, the pope continued, an *efficiently socialized division of labor* became the only criterion for economic organization.

---

[31] Pars. 111-113.

[32] Par. 113.

[33] Par. 118. The discussion of Socialism encompasses pars. 111-123.

As a result, people were required "to surrender themselves entirely to society," including if necessary their liberty, and there was no place for "true social authority, which ... descends from God alone, the Creator and last end of all." Therefore, he again proclaimed, "no one can be at the same time a good Catholic and a true socialist."[34]

Pius XI continued his condemnation of Socialism by warning of "a certain new kind of socialist activity" that attempts to pervade "morality and culture," that seeks to train "the mind and character," and that in particular aims a "children of a tender age."

He then repeated the now classical papal social analysis of a slippery slope from the modern European Enlightenment of Liberalism into Communism: "Let all remember that Liberalism (Capitalism) is the father of this Socialism that is pervading morality and culture, and that Bolshevism will be its heir."[35]

The pope concluded his reflections on Socialism by lamenting that "not a few of Our sons ... have gone over to the ranks of Socialism." He rejected the excuse that the Church had abandoned the poor, and pointed to the great legacy of Leo's encyclical on labor. Then he invited those who had left the Church for Socialism to return.[36]

Spiritual Root of the Crisis

For Pius XI, the "ardently desired social restoration" could only proceed from "a renewal of the Christian spirit." In his analysis, "the present economic system" (Liberal Capitalism) labored "un-

---

[34] Pars. 118-120.

[35] Pars. 121-122.

[36] Pars. 123-126.

der the gravest of evils," while "Communism and Socialism" had wandered "far from the precepts of the Gospel." "Only a return to Christian life and institutions" could heal society. So serious was the crisis, he said, that it threatened the "loss of souls."[37]

The root cause of the crisis of economic and social life, and of the resulting "apostasy of great numbers of Christian workers from the faith," was, he argued, "the *disordered passions* of the soul," which are the "result of original sin." These "disordered passions" have expressed themselves as an *"unquenchable thirst for riches and temporal goods,* which has at times impelled men to break God's laws and trample on the rights of their neighbors." (Italics added.) Such "disordered passion" had always been present to some degree, but the pope saw them as acutely aggravated by the "present system of economic life."[38]

The easy gains that a market unrestricted by any law opens to everybody attracts large numbers to buying and selling goods, and they, their one aim being to make quick profits with the least expenditure of work, raise or lower prices by their uncontrolled business dealings so rapidly according to their own caprice and greed that they nullify the wisest forecasts of producers.

The laws passed to promote corporate business, while dividing and limiting the risk of business, have given occasion to the most sordid license. For We observe that consciences are little affected by this reduced obligation of accountability; that furthermore, by hiding under the shelter of a joint name, the worse of injustices and frauds are perpetrated; that that, too, directors of business

---

[37] Pars. 127-131.

[38] Par. 132.

companies, forgetful of their trust, betray the rights of those whose savings they have undertaken to administer.

Lastly, We must not omit to mention those crafty men who, wholly unconcerned about any honesty usefulness of their work, do not scruple to stimulate the baser human desires and, when they are aroused, use them for their own profits.[39]

Such economic license emerged, the pope claimed, precisely because the "new form of economic life" arose along with "the principles of rationalism," which then created "a body of economic teaching far removed from the true moral law." As a result, he continued, "completely free rein was given to human passions."

Thus, for Pius XI, the spiritual and moral crisis at the root of the modern social question was *the direct fruit of the applications of Enlightenment rationalism to the economic arena.* Then, when the "rulers of economic life" charted a destructive course, "the rank and file of workers everywhere" rushed "headlong into the same chasm, and all the more so, because very many managers treated their workers like mere tools, with no concern at all for their souls."[40]

The solution, the pope proclaimed, is to return to the teaching of the Gospels, which the Church preaches. "All created goods under God (need to be) considered as mere instruments to be used only in so far as they conduce to the attainment of the supreme end." He continued, "The *sordid love of wealth,* which is the shame and great sin of our age, will be opposed ... by the gentle yet effective law of Christian moderation" (italics added).[41]

---

[39] Par. 132.

[40] Pars. 133-135.

[41] Par. 136.

Conclusion

Finally, the pope insisted that justice, while essential, could not do without *charity*. Justice, he argued, can "remove the causes of social conflict," but only charity can "*bring about the union of hearts and minds*" (italics added). Such was the perspective that needed to guide his "restoration of human society in Christ."

He rejoiced that "workers themselves" were taking up this challenge. He appealed through the clergy to "lay apostles of both workers and employers" for all to take up "an intensive study of the social question," to form "Christian organizations" and "study groups guided by principles in harmony with the Faith," to promote "Workers' Retreats," and for all to be united "under the leadership and guidance of the Church."

He urged everyone "to contribute ... to the Christian reconstruction of human society which Leo XIII inaugurated through his immortal encyclical, *On the Condition of Workers*."[42]

---

[42] Pars. 137-147.

MATER ET MAGISTRA

"On Christianity and Social Progress"
1961 Social Encyclical of John XXIII
Written for the 60ᵗʰ Anniversary of Rerum Novarum

An excerpt from a book in preparation by Joe Holland and tentatively titled
THE PROPHETIC VISION OF BLESSED JOHN XXIII:
FOUNDER OF POSTMODERN CATHOLIC SOCIAL TEACHING
FOR THE NEW GLOBAL ERA, 1958-1963
(Forthcoming from Pacem in Terris Press in 2012)

In 1961, on the 70ᵗʰ anniversary of RERUM NOVARUM, John XXIII (1958-1963) issued his famous encyclical, MATER ET MAGISTRA (Mother and Teacher), carrying the subtitle *"On Christianity and Social Progress."*

With the French Dominican priest Louis-Joseph Lebret reportedly its primary drafter, the document was an extensive reflection on human work in the context of agriculture, global development, and the new "socialization." The document may be seen as the first papal social encyclical of the new global postmodern stage of Catholic Social Teaching.[43]

---

[43] The official English text may be found on the website of the Vatican at:

Again, issued seventy years after RERUM NOVARUM, this encyclical first reviewed the social teachings of Leo XIII, Pius XI, and Pius XII (in his famous Pentecost 1941 radio address on the 50th anniversary of RERUM NOVARUM). John's document then attempted to "confirm and make more specific their teachings, as well as to determine more clearly the mind of the Church on the new and important problems of the day."[44]

Because of this encyclical's *bold new vision for the world economic order*, we need to review its teachings in some detail.

The document's overall structure for these teachings is as follows:[45]

- Introduction

- Part One: Teaching of RERUM NOVARUM and Development by Pius XI and Pius XII

- Part Two: Clarifications and Developments Added to the Teachings of RERUM NOVARUM

- Part Three: New Aspects of the Social Question

- Part Four: Renewing the Ties of Common Life in Truth, Justice, and Love

---

http://www.vatican.va/holy_father/john_xxiii/encyclicals/documents/hf_j-xxiii_enc_15051961_mater_en.html (accessed 2012-05-01).

[44] Par. 50.

[45] The official French version may be the original text, since the reported main writer, Lebret, a native of France, would have done his drafting in French. Assuming that this is true, I will largely use the headings found in the French version, because they differ significantly from those found in the official English version. The French version may be found on the Vatican website at: *http://www.vatican.va/holy_father/john_xxiii/encyclicals/documents/hf_j-xxiii_enc_15051961_mater_fr.html* (accessed 2015-05-01).

Introduction

Addressing his encyclical to bishops at all levels as was customary, and also to other clergy as was frequent, John (in an unusual turn) also directed this document to all the "Faithful of the entire Catholic World." He then reminded his readers that the Church is "Mother and Teacher" of all nations and addresses the whole person, "body and soul."

He pointed out the Church's concern with "temporal welfare and prosperity," and Jesus' compassion for the multitude by providing "bread for the body" as well as "food for the soul" – mentioning here the two-thousand year old ministrations of "deacons."[46]

After recalling how Jesus was concerned not only with people's souls, but also with their material welfare, again for example in "the hunger of the crowds," John emphasized the achievements of RERUM NOVARUM and its subsequent impact.

Leo XIII's famous encyclical opened, he stated, "new horizons for the activity of the universal Church," and it made him "the champion and restorer" of the rights of the "lowly and oppressed."

He described RERUM NOVARUM as "that magnificent encyclical on the conditions of the working classes" and highlighted the influence it has had on governmental legislation.

Referring to its "permanent validity," he then turned to the document itself.[47]

---

[46] Pars. 1-6.

[47] Pars. 7-9.

Part I.

Teachings of the Encyclical Rerum Novarum and its Development in the Magisterium of Pius XI and Pius XII

Epoch of the Encyclical 'Rerum Novarum'

John described Leo's time as one of "social and economic upheaval, of heightening tensions and actual revolt," with the denial of "any correlation between economics and morality." The only rule, he wrote, was that of "free and unrestricted competition," with the laws of market seen as something "*mechanical*" (italics added).[48] As a result, wages were often insufficient, even forcing people into starvation, and they were likewise "injurious to health, morality, and religious faith." In addition, "extremist theories" threatened "far worse" damage. Interestingly, he did not explicitly mention Socialism by name, though resistance against it had been at the center of Leo's strategy.[49]

Pathways of Reconstruction

John then summarized Leo's "complete synthesis of social principles," which, he claimed, were formulated with great "historical insight." In contrast to those who had been preaching "resignation to the poor and generosity to the rich," Leo insisted that there was no solution to the socio-economic crisis without "the counsel of religion and of the Church." The Church provided the moral articulation of "basic economic and social principles for the recon-

---

[48] The term *mechanical* is a reference to the erroneous philosophical anthropology and cosmology of Liberal Capitalism.

[49] Pars. 8-15.

struction of human society." Summarizing John material, these principles may be described as follows.

- *Human Work.* Work is not "a commodity," but "a human activity" for which "remuneration" cannot depend on the state nor the market, but rather on "the laws of justice and equity."

- *Private Property.* "Private ownership of property, including productive goods, is a natural right which the state cannot suppress," but "it naturally entails a social obligation."

- *The State.* The purpose of the state is "the realization of the common good," and so it cannot "hold aloof from economic matters," but rather must "promote the production of a sufficient supply of material goods." It has "the duty to protect the rights of all its members, the workers, women and children."

- *Terms of Employment.* The state also needs to regulate "the terms of employment" according to "justice and equity," including safeguarding the work environment both materially and spiritually, with this role later expanded as "labor law."

- *Workers' Associations. Workers have the "natural right to enter into association"* (italics added), either as workers alone or with employers, as well as to work freely and without hindrance within these associations.

- *Ideologies.* "Workers and employers should regulate their mutual relations in accordance with the principle of human solidarity and Christian brotherhood." Both unrestricted competition in the sense of Liberal Capitalism, and the Marxist creed of class warfare, are contrary to Christian teaching and human nature.

John described these principles as the *"Magna Charta"* of social and economic reconstruction.[50]

Encyclical Quadragesimo Anno

Next the document summarized the clarifying contributions of Pius XI in his 1931 encyclical, QUADRAGESIMO ANNO. It did this in regard to the issues of private property, the wage system, and moderate Socialism, as well as the new economic concentration.

- *Private Property.* Pius XI enlarged on the "social aspect" of private property and on the "obligations of ownership."

- *Wage System.* Pius XI defended the justice of the wage system but condemned its unjust implementation, and specified terms and conditions for just and equitable use of it. He further advised modifying the wage system by allowing "employees to participate in the ownership or the management, or in some way share in the profits." In addition, he stated:

  > ... justice demands that account be taken not only of the needs of the individual workers and their families, but also of the financial state of the business concern for which they work and of the economic welfare of the whole people.[51]

- *Moderate Socialism.* Pius XI "made it clear that no Catholic could subscribe even to moderate Socialism," since its doctrine is based only on "material well-being ... aims solely at production ... places too severe a restraint on human liberty, and flouts the true notion of social authority."

---

[50] Pars. 15-26 for these principles.

[51] Pars. 27-36.

- *Economic Concentration.* Yet Pius XI also condemned the "liberal" experience which "concentrated a despotic economic power in the hands of a few," and the fact that "economic domination has taken the place of the open market," with "even the public authority becoming a tool of *plutocracy* (italics added), which was thus gaining a stranglehold on the entire world."

Then John told how Pius XI responded to these crises by means of three proposals.

- *Common Good.* All interests need to be subordinated to the common good.

- *Vocational Bodies.* There needs to be created "economic and vocational bodies which would be autonomous and independent of the State."

- *World Order.* There is need to begin a world-scale cooperation for the "economic welfare of all nations" This third proposal requires that there be created "a national and international juridical order" with a "network of public and private institutions" aimed at serving "the common good."[52]

Radio Message of Pentecost 1941

Finally, John summarized the social teaching of Pius XII in that pope's Pentecost Sunday radio message of 1 June 1941, again marking the 50th anniversary of RERUM NOVARUM.[53] According to John, Pius XII made three major contributions in this address.

---

52 Pars. 37-40.

53 Pius XII issued no social encyclicals, but instead used what he called the "Marconi Radio" to issue multiple social statements, most famously his

- *Universal Destiny of Material Goods.* The right of every person to use material goods is "prior to every other economic right, including that of private property," since "the goods which were created by God for all ... should flow to all alike, according to the principles of justice and charity."

- *State's Role in Employment.* If the activity of individuals is not sufficient to create work for all, then it falls "back on the State to intervene in the division and distribution of work," according to the common good.

- *Right to Migration.* Families have the freedom to migrate, in order that "the father of a family" might secure "the healthy liberty he needs in order to fulfill the duties assigned him by the creation regarding the physical, spiritual and religious welfare of the family." (Here the patriarchal model of family is still considered normative.)[54]

Recent Changes

Next John noted the *"radical transformation"* (italics added) which "the economic scene had undergone" during the past twenty years (1941-1961) since Pius XII's radio message, both in the internal structure of states and in the relations of states with each other. In this "radical transformation," by which John in effect acknowledged *a new stage of modern industrial society*, he referred to three clusters of changes.

Christmas messages. This was Pius' attempts to embrace the new medium. Unfortunately, however, his words over radio waves are less remembered than the published social documents of other popes.

[54] Pars. 41-45 for these three contributions.

- *Scientific, Technological, Economic Transformations.* John's examples included nuclear energy, chemical manufacture of synthetics, automation in industry and public services, modernization of agriculture, new electronic communications (radio and television), and rapid transportation including initial steps toward the "conquest of interplanetary space."

- *Social Transformations.* In *positive* terms, there was social insurance and social security systems, maturing of labor unions, advancement in education and wider distribution of consumer goods leading to a breakdown of class barriers, as well as wider interest in global public life by ordinary citizens. In *negative* terms, there were imbalances between agriculture on one side and industry and public services on the other, as well as within political communities, and a "marked disparity in the economic wealth possessed by different countries."

- *Political Transformations.* Here there appeared the "breakaway from colonialism and the attainment of political independence by the peoples of Asia and Africa," and "an ever-extending network of societies and organizations (which) concentrate on the economic, social, cultural and political welfare of all nations throughout the world."[55]

Themes of the New Encyclical

John then explained the *two aims* of his new encyclical: 1) *to confirm and clarify specific the teachings of (his) Predecessors (Leo XIII, Pius XI, and Pius XII); and 2) to determine clearly the mind of the Church on the new and important problems of the day.*[56]

---

[55] Pars. 46-49.

[56] Par. 50.

Part II.
Clarifications and Developments Contributed to the Teachings of Rerum Novarum

John began Part Two by seeking to fulfill his first goal: again, "to confirm and clarify the teachings" of Leo XIII, Pius XI, and Pius XII for contemporary times. The areas he addressed are:

- the expanded role of the *state*
- the new concept of *socialization*
- expanded principles regarding *justice* in human work

Personal Initiative and Government Intervention in Economic Matters

Regarding the state, while recognizing that "in the economic order first place must be given to the personal initiative of private citizens working as individuals or in association," John argued that "the civil power must have a hand in the economy." It does this, he proposed, in three ways:

- *Guidance* - by promoting production through "directing, stimulating, coordinating, supplying, and integrating," all according to the guiding "principle of subsidiary function;"

- *Imbalances* - by using the "present advance in scientific knowledge and productive Technology" to reduce, "to a much greater degree than ever before," the "imbalances" which exist within branches of the economy, within regions of a country, and among "the different peoples of the world," and to do this by "limiting fluctuations in the economy," preventing "mass unemployment," and generally increasing "the degree and scope" of its activities;

- *Freedom* - by never "depriving the individual citizen of freedom of action," and especially support of family and "the free development of productive activity;" otherwise, "political tyranny ensues and, in addition, economic stagnation."[57]

Socialization:
Origin, Magnitude, and Assessment of the Phenomenon

Regarding the new concept called *socialization*, John noted that "one of the principal characteristics which seems to be typical of our age is an increase in social relationships" through "the introduction of many and varied forms of associations." This was due, he claimed, to "scientific and technical progress, greater productive efficiency, and a higher standard of living." While some readers thought John's reference to expanded "socialization" meant Socialism, he was rather attempting to draw the Catholic tradition toward a greater understanding of the social side of human existence, while avoiding the atheism and materialism of the socialist ideology. Yet such a move would support significant common ground with socialists in pursuit of social justice.[58]

John described this socialization as the reason for the *"growing intervention of the State."* He noted "many advantages" of this state-intervention in supporting human rights and participation. He also linked this development to the new means of communications. The progressive perfection of modern methods of thought diffusion - the press, cinema, radio, television – makes it possible,

---

[57] Pars. 51-58.

[58] On this papal opening to Socialism, see Michael J. Schuck, THAT THEY BE ONE: THE SOCIAL TEACHINGS OF THE PAPAL ENCYCLICALS 1740-1989 (Washington DC: Georgetown University Press, 1991), p. 171, n. 104.

he argued, for everyone to participate in human events the world over.[59]

John then noted that this also led to "a multiplicity of restrictive laws and regulations in many departments of human life," which "narrows the sphere of a person's freedom of action." Yet, he insisted, this need not reduce people to "the condition of being mere automatons." Rather these new conditions could be realized in a way that would diminish the disadvantages while supporting the advantages. For this to happen, however, there was required a clear view of the common good by the public authority, as well as for the various "intermediate bodies and corporate enterprise" to collaborate to form "a true community," guided by "the moral order." John's name for this whole process, taken from Pius XI, was *"organic reconstruction."*[60]

Remuneration for Work:
Norms of Justice and Equity

Regarding human work, John began globally with the "developing countries" and told how he was "filled with an overwhelming sadness" over ... "the millions of workers in many lands and entire continents condemned through the inadequacy of their wages to live with their families in utterly sub-human conditions."[61]

While he felt this was "probably due to the fact that the process of industrialization in these countries was only in its initial stages," he nevertheless decried the "enormous wealth, the unbridled luxury, of the privileged few (which) stands in violent, offensive con-

---

[59] Pars. 59-61.

[60] Pars. 62-67.

[61] Pars. 68-70.

trast to the utter poverty of the vast majority." He decried "the vast sums spent on armaments." In the "developed countries," he lamented the high remuneration for "relatively unimportant services, and services of doubtful value, while the diligent and profitable work of whole classes of honest, hard-working men get scant reward, which is inadequate to meet the basic needs of life."[62]

Clearly, John accepted here a benevolent view of the overall process of industrialization as laying the foundation for human prosperity, even if he did not see its fruits as fairly distributed. His earlier warning about the *marginalization of labor* through automation, however, was not integrated with this underlying benevolent view. Further, there was no explicit reflection on the industrialization's impending *ecological crisis*, soon to appear threateningly on the horizon, though his concern with "balance" for agriculture may be interpreted as an early papal expression of support for *agro-ecology*.

Principles for Human Work

Next, John articulated the principles regarding human work which he wished to confirm and further specify. This section of the encyclical is quite long, and it would be impossible to do it justice in the space of a single chapter. So I will try here simply to extract the *key principles* named by John. For a full understanding of the material, the reader is referred to the encyclical itself.

- *Wages.* Wages cannot be left to the laws of the market, or to the will of the powerful. Rather employers should pay a just and family wage, though "other factors" also need to be taken into account; for example, individual achievement, the state of

---

[62] Pars. 68-70.

the company and the country, the common good of *the universal family of nations,* and the available natural resources.

- **Sharing in Productivity.** "Economic progress must be accompanied by a corresponding social progress," whereby all citizens "participate in the increased productivity," including shares in the firm for workers.

- **Common Good.** Wages and profits need to be determined in light of the common good: at the national level by avoiding privileged classes and fostering balance between all economic sectors (agriculture, industry, and services); and at the international level by avoiding unfair competition and fostering "development of the economically less advanced countries."

- **Working Conditions.** Work is an opportunity for human self-expression, so working conditions must protect human dignity, responsibility, and personal initiative.

- **Scale of Work.** "Small and average sized undertakings in agriculture, in the arts and crafts, in commerce and industry should be fostered," including "cooperative associations" and in large firms "contract of work by partnership." Special state support is due to "artisan and cooperative enterprises." In a long section here on small-scale cooperatives, the hand of LeBret, so devoted to economic cooperatives, seems obvious.

- **Workers' Participation in Management.** Workers are not "cogs in the machinery," but need to have a say in "the efficient running and development of the enterprise," particularly in light of their greater skill and longer schooling.

- **Workers' Associations and Public Decisions.** Given the growth and legal recognition of workers associations, these bodies should participate in the discussions of public authorities regarding the economy as a whole. Here John expressed great praise for "Christian workers associations" (Catholic inspired 'Christian Democratic' trade unions) and for the "United Nations International Labor Organization" (ILO).[63]

- *Large Enterprises and Common Good.* Public authority must guide large enterprises toward the common good. Sometimes this need is addressed through systems of social insurance and social security.

- *Knowledge Workers.* Today some people are "aiming at proficiency in their trade or profession, rather than the acquisition of private property." This shows that work is an expression of the person and "must always be rated higher than the possession of external goods, which are merely instrumental." John saw this as an advance in our civilization. This point reflects the dawn of the information age, and of the new class of knowledge workers.

- *Right of Ownership.* Since the individual is prior to society, private ownership and even productive goods are part of the natural order and indispensable for free and personal initiative in the economic field. Hence the need to harmonize justice and

---

[63] Actually, the ILO was founded in the early twentieth century as part of the League of Nations, well before the creation of the United Nations, and partly out of inspiration by Catholic Social Teaching. In testimony to that inspiration, there was traditionally been a Jesuit priest on the staff of the ILO. See the fascinating narrative by the Joseph Joblin, SJ, the 'ILO Jesuit' from 1956 to 1981: "Eighty Years of Jesuit Presence in the International Labor Movement," found at: *http://www.sjweb.info/sjs/pjold/pj_show.cfm?PubTextID=1544* (accessed 2012-05-01). I had the honor of collaborating in various projects with Père Joblin, as well as with his American successor, John Lucal, SJ, who was the 'ILO Jesuit' from 1981 to 1986.

freedom. Yet John cannot have meant here prior in the order of time but rather prior in the order of dignity, since Catholic Social Teaching had consistently rejected a social-contract theory of society (in which supposedly autonomous individuals are seen as form a society only by contract). The Catholic social tradition has always had insisted that humans were from the beginning and by nature social creatures. Also, John noted, movements formerly opposed to private property, presumably socialist, are now "declaring themselves in favor of this right."

- *Wages and Productivity.* Within limits of the common good, as productivity increases, so too should wages.

- *Distribution of Property.* Not only the right, but also the fact of private property needs to be extended to all classes of citizens, and all the more so today.

- *Public Ownership.* Also especially today as the common good becomes more complex, the state or the public may also own productive goods, particularly when leaving their ownership in private hands would cause injury to the community at large,

- *Subsidiarity.* As state and public ownership necessarily increases, it is important to remember the principle of subsidiarity which requires that the role of the state and other public agencies always be limited only to what is necessary for the common good. Careful checks should be exercised over the character of those entrusted with this responsibility, and over the degree of concentration of state power.

- *Social Function of Property.* The right of private property has an inherently social function, for it is "the plan of the Creator (that) all of the world's goods are primarily intended for the worthy support of the entire human race." An owner is but "steward of God's Providence, for the benefit of others."

- **Personal Charity.** In spite of the growth of public programs, "a vast field" remains "for the exercise of human sympathy and the Christian charity of individuals, as well as of groups." Indeed, "the divine Master frequently extends to the rich the insistent invitation to convert their material goods into spiritual ones by conferring them on the poor."[64]

Part III.
New Aspects of the Social Question

Next John turned to his second principal aim, namely "to determine the mind of the Church on the new and important problems of the day."[65]

He pointed out that *the social question can no longer be seen primarily as the relationship between worker and mangers.* Rather, he stated, it now also needed to include two other dimensions: 1) the relationship between different *sectors* of the economic, and specifically the underdevelopment of agriculture (in terms of human participation); and 2) the relationship between different *countries* in the world within the overall development process, with different countries having different degrees of economic and social development.[66]

Thus, his two new themes were:

---

[64] Pars. 71-121.

[65] Par. 50.

[66] Par. 122.

- Imbalanced underdevelopment of *agriculture*
- Imbalanced development among *countries*, with many countries still highly underdeveloped

Both issues represented an expansion of the focus from the prior orientation of Catholic Social Teaching almost exclusively to the urban class relationship between industrial capital and industrial labor, which normally meant in the center countries industrialized world.

The expanded orientation called for by John addressed imbalances between "various branches of the economy," both within nations and between nations. This was the complementing of concern about *labor* (a class perspective) with concern about sectoral and national *development*, with all set in a *global* framework. This expansion of focus marked *the birth of a new global and rural-urban stage* within Catholic Social Teaching concerning what it has called "the social question."

The need for this expansion of focus arose with the birth of the new *Global Capitalism*. Due to the growing global networks of transportation and communications flowing from the Electronic Revolution, capital was beginning to move out of the older industrial areas to 'less developed' regions of the center countries and even to 'less developed' countries of the planet. Further, agricultural workers were increasingly being displaced from the land and were increasingly forced to relocate in expanding urban areas.

These two transformations would eventually lead to a great destabilization of the economic, political, and cultural life of the old industrial regions in the countries of the system's center, and, of course, also in the peripheral agricultural areas and in peripheral countries.

Eventually these issues would create a more radical awareness of a deeper *ecological crisis* of the very industrial paradigm itself. During John's time, however, that deeper paradigm crisis not yet been widely foreseen. For the moment, the new global movement of capital was still widely seen as an extension of the mature industrial system in the center countries. That extension was then given the name "development." Given that framework, John began with his first theme of agriculture.

Demands of Justice
in the Agricultural Sectors

The child of farmers, John noted that agriculture was becoming depressed, as more people moved out of farming and into the cities. In addressing this issue, he raised the following questions:

What can be done to reduce the disproportion in productive efficiency between agriculture on the one hand, and industry and services on the other; and to ensure that agricultural living standards approximate as closely as possible those enjoyed by city-dwellers who draw their resources either from industry or from services in which they are engaged?

What can be done to persuade agricultural workers that, far from being inferior to other people, they have every opportunity of developing their personality through their work, and can look forward to the future with confidence?[67]

To resolve the imbalanced approach to development which so neglected agriculture, and also to address the distressed state of agricultural workers, John recommended a series of pro-

---

[67] Par. 125.

agricultural policies. As before, this section is again too extensive to fully report here. So I will simply list John's key recommendations:

- Infrastructure in agricultural areas (roads, schools, etc.)
- Gradual development which deliberately keeps agriculture in balance with industry
- Tax policies which support agriculture
- Credit policies and credit banks providing capital at moderate interest rates
- Special social insurance programs taking into account the Low income of agricultural workers
- Price supports for agricultural products
- Locating industries related to agriculture in agricultural regions
- Supporting the family farm as the ideal model
- Systems of instruction and cooperatives to aid family farms
- Allowing citizens in rural areas to lead in their own development
- Supporting and assisting rural private enterprise
- Attempting to keep a balance between land and population
- Freer movement of goods, capital, and people across national borders [68]

Overall John was proposing that modern human development preserve its roots in the land and the family farm, again an experience very precious to him from his own childhood memories of growing up on a family farm.

Later this would be accepted by many more as also a wise and even necessary ecological strategy, though John himself did not

---

[68] Pars. 127-147.

use the word 'ecological.' In most countries, however, development was, as noted, still pressing people in the opposite urbanized
and anti-ecological direction.

Imbalance of Underdevelopment
In the Developing Nations

John then moved to his other new theme, the imbalanced economic relationship between "political communities that are economically advanced and those in the process of development." In the
name of human solidarity and describing himself as "the father of
all peoples," and still later in the name of the "Mystical Body of
Christ," he appealed to the "wealthy nations" to come to the aid of
those nations suffering from "hunger, misery, and poverty." He
suggested that, without overcoming these imbalances, there
would be no lasting world peace.[69]

Then John made extensive proposals for how development could
be advance in conformity with a truly human vision, and also in
conformity with Christian teachings. Again, the material here is
vast, and so I will once more simply list tersely the policies that
John recommended in the name of development:

- International aid from the countries with excess consumer
  goods
- Scientific, technical and professional training by international
  and national organizations, including "world banking insti-
  tutes" (all of which, he said, are "a magnificent work")
- Developing nations learning from the experience of the weal-
  thier nations

---

[69] Pars. 157-159.

- Balance among agriculture, industry, and service sectors
- Respecting the traditions of developing nations
- Giving aid without any attempt to dominate
- Preserving the true "hierarchy of values" in which Science, Technology, and economics are only instrumental to the spiritual[70]

In all of this, John again did not speak of a 'Christian Civilization,' but rather of *"true civilization"* which he saw as *"humanistic"* (italics added). Nonetheless, he celebrated the role of the Church in this new world-historical moment. Supporting the new cultural diversity arising to human consciousness across the globe in this post-colonial era, John insisted that the Church in its internal life "does not aim at uniformity," but only at "unity." He also praised the role of Catholic citizens working to support development.[71]

Population, Family, and the Transmission of Life

In his section on development, John also addressed the emerging question of population growth, which he recognized as "a world problem, as well as one especially for the poverty-stricken nations." Despite dire predictions of population growth exceeding economic growth and soon outstripping food supply, John expressed his doubt that such a threat was imminent. He saw the problem more a maldistribution of resources, in part due to underdevelopment.[72]

---

[70] Pars. 161-176.

[71] Pars. 177-184.

[72] Pars. 185-192.

Here John also addressed the theme of family and the transmission of life. As one would expect, he supported the family as the place for this transmission, and he defended the sacred character of human life. For this reason, he said, it was not permitted to use "certain ways and means which are allowable in the propagation of plant and animal life." But he was not specific. Nonetheless, he did acknowledge that there was a serious population problem, and he indicated his belief that "a provident God (will grant) sufficient means to the human race to find a dignified solution to the problems attendant upon the transmission of life."[73]

Arms Race and Underdevelopment

Then John turned to yet another major issue, this time negatively linked to development, namely the arms race.

Here he lamented that, while Science and Technology had brought a closer relationship between nations, these same nations still feared conquest and were busy building up "munitions of war as a deterrent against the would-be aggressor ... The result," he wrote, was "a vast expenditure of human energy and natural resources on projects which are disruptive of human society."

He claimed that "the root cause (was) the presence of ideological differences between nations".[74] John's solution was mutual recognition of the moral order, but he added that the moral order cannot be sustained without acknowledgment of its source in God.

John insisted that the ultimate solution to our great social problems was God, "the Creator and Ruler of man and his world."

---

[73] Pars. 193-199.

[74] Pars. 200-206.

Without God, he argued, we are headed for destruction already apparent in "the increasing sense of dissatisfaction with worldly goods," which is even now undermining the "illusion of an earthly paradise."

Hence, modern humans need to become aware of "limitations" and to create "a striving for spiritual values." Thus John set the stage for his concluding section on the need for a new social order at both the national and international levels.[75]

Part IV.
Renewing the Bonds of Life in Common according to Truth, Justice, and Love

Reductionist and Erroneous Ideologies

Now, toward the end of his encyclical, John defined what he saw as the main problem:

> *After all this scientific and technical progress, and even because of it, the problem remains: how to build up a new order of society based on a more balanced human relationship between political communities on a national and international level.*[76]

Modern ideologies had failed in their attempt, John stated, because they did not "take into account the whole person." (Though he did not mention them by name, the two dominant modern ideologies are Liberal Capitalism and Scientific Socialism.) In this regard, he continued that the most fundamental error was to imagine that

---

[75] Pars. 207-210.

[76] Par. 212.

... humanity's natural sense of religion is nothing else than the outcome of feeling or fantasy, to be eradicated from his soul as an anachronism and an obstacle to human progress.[77]

Hence, John argued, "there will be no peace or justice in the world until (people) return to a sense of their dignity as creatures and sons of God." The modern era, he continued, perniciously attempted "to reconstruct a solid and fruitful temporal order divorced from God," and "to eliminate the soul's upward surge toward God." In the words of Scripture, "unless the Lord build the house, they labor in vain who build it."[78]

Eternal Timeliness of the Social Doctrine of the Church, the 'See-Judge-Act' Method, and Centrality of the Laity

This modern crisis, John stated, showed the abiding validity of the Church's Social Doctrine. Among its most fundamental principles, he stated, were the teaching that:

- Individual *human persons* are the foundation, the cause, and the end of every social institution

- This is because human persons are by nature *social beings*

- By the plan of Providence, they are raised to an order of reality which is *above nature.*[79]

It was essential, John insisted, that this social doctrine be widely diffused not only among Catholics, but also among "people of good will everywhere." It should be taught in all Catholic educa-

---

[77] Par. 214

[78] Pars. 214-217; PSALM 126, Verse1.

[79] Pars. 218-220.

tional institutions, in parishes, and in the "Lay Apostolate," and then "translated into reality," so as to combat the "deep-rooted selfishness ... materialism ... (and) hedonism" of modern society.[80]

Further, John commended the 'SEE-JUDGE-ACT' methodology that the Belgian priest Joseph Cardijn had developed in his movement of Young Christian Workers (YCW) during the first half of the twentieth century. This method was eventually widely used in a range of Catholic Action movements.

> *There are three stages which should normally be followed in the reduction of social principles into practice. First, one reviews the concrete situation; secondly, one forms a judgment on it in the light of these same principles; thirdly, one decides what in the circumstances can and should be done to implement these principles. These are the three stages that are usually expressed in the three terms: look, judge, act. It is important for our young people to grasp this method and to practice it.*[81]

This three-stage method – beginning with a *social analysis*, then moving to a *biblical-theological reflection* on the situation, and finally recommending a *strategic response* to the situation – is found in the structure of most of papal encyclicals since the tradition's origin in 1740, and it largely continues up to the present. So, while the method became famous with Cardijn, it is far older.

But the assumptions and content of the three steps of social analysis, theological reflection, and strategic planning were quite different in the Pre-Leonine papal strategy (from 1740-1878), and different again in Leonine papal strategy (1878-1958), as they are also

---

[80] Pars. 221-235.

[81] Pars. 236-237.

different here in this foundational vision of the Johannine strategy (1958 ...). Thus the method does not of itself determine the content, which can vary dramatically.

For example, soon after John's Vatican Council II, the three-step method would again appear in the more radical form of Liberation Theology, using a radically Mosaic theological paradigm that the one that had reigned with the Davidic theological paradigm used which legitimated the aristocratic class structure of classical Christian Civilization.[82]

John added that all this needed to happen under the direction of the bishops, but that it was the particular task of "our sons (and daughters), the laity" – still non-inclusive language but no longer 'children' – to live "an active life in the world and organize themselves for the attainment of temporal ends." Otherwise, he said, the people of this age would lose "their own identity in their works, which they admire to the point of idolatry."

After a statement commending Sunday rest, John returned to the theme of the laity, and argued that the active life was not incompatible with spiritual perfection, and that in fact "a person should develop and perfect oneself through one's daily work." The ultimate task, John continued, is "to create a contemporary (global) civilization advancing according to criteria of authentic humanism

---

[82] For a reflection on the sources and development of this method, see Joe Holland, "Roots of the Pastoral Circle in Personal Experiences and Catholic Tradition," in Frans Wijsen, Peter Henriot, & Rodrigo Mejía, editors, THE PASTORAL CIRCLE REVISITED: A CRITICAL QUEST FOR TRUTH AND TRANSFORMATION (Maryknoll NY: Orbis Books, 2005). In addition, a model for use of the method, and especially the first step, can be found in my book with Peter Henriot, SJ, SOCIAL ANALYSIS: LINKING FAITH AND JUSTICE, Revised Edition (Orbis Books, 1983).

and of evangelical teachings,"[83] and to "help to bring about a realization of Christ's kingdom in this world." He added that this is to be done through the laity in their work. So significant is this statement that it may be helpful to cite here John's full text:

> *That a person should develop and perfect oneself through one's daily work—which in most cases is of a temporal character—is perfectly in keeping with the plan of divine Providence. The Church today is faced with an immense task: to building the civilization of this age by advancing the norms of true humanity and of evangelical teachings. The continued development of this civilization, indeed its very survival, demand and insist that the Church do her part in the world.*
>
> *That is why, as We said before, she claims the co-operation of her laity. In conducting their human affairs to the best of their ability, they must recognize that they are doing a service to humanity, in intimate union with God through Christ, and to God's greater glory. And St. Paul insisted: "Whether you eat or drink, or whatsoever else you do, do all to the glory of God." (1 Corinthians 10:31) "All whatsoever you do in word or in work, do all in the name of the Lord Jesus Christ, giving thanks to God (Colossians 3:17).*[84]

---

[83] I have re-translated here part of the official English version of John's statement in this par. 256. This part of the English version reads: *to humanize and to Christianize this modern civilization of ours.* But the Latin version does not use the phrase *modern civilization.* Rather, it speaks of a *civilization of this age.* Also, the English version could be read as calling for a 'Christian Civilization.' But the Latin version literally calls for the Church *to build the civilization of this age advancing the norms of true humanity and of evangelical teachings.* The context, of course, shows that John was referring to a global civilization.

[84] Pars. 248-261.

John's vision here is for the Church, and especially the laity through their work, to serve the new Global Civilization not by creating a confessionally Christian Civilization, but rather by advancing a humanistic World Civilization based justice and peace, which are criteria that converge with evangelical teachings, and which in turn will open the hearts and minds of human persons to the truth of the Gospel and thereby help to reveal the Kingdom of God.

The full and ultimate coming of the Kingdom of God is, of course, eschatological. But seeking the Kingdom of God only in the *Eschaton* and not also attempting to make it present at least partially in this world, is not authentic Catholic teaching. If it were, then Catholic Social Teaching would never have the centrality that it does.

This was made clear by the subsequent 1971 World Synod of Bishops in its document JUSTICE IN THE WORLD, which stated that action for justice and transformation of the world is a *"constitutive dimension of the preaching of the Gospel."* Because of the importance of this statement, it may be helpful to cite the full section from the Synodal text:

> *The uncertainty of history and the painful convergences in the ascending path of the human community direct us to sacred history; there God has revealed himself to us, and made known to us, as it is brought progressively to realization, his plan of liberation and salvation which is once and for all fulfilled in the Paschal Mystery of Christ.*
>
> *Action on behalf of justice and participation in the transformation of the world fully appear to us as a **constitutive** dimension of the preaching of the Gospel, or, in other words, of the Church's mis-*

sion for the redemption of the human race and its liberation from
every oppressive situation (bold added).[85]

In his conclusion, John repeated his theme that "the Catholic and Apostolic Church is the Mother and Teacher of all nations," and that through the Lord, in the language of Psalm 64, justice and peace would kiss.[86]

Significance of Mater et Magistra

The strength of MATER ET MAGISTRA was that in it John officially recognized the new moment of social history now known as Global Capitalism, which provided the technological foundation (but not the ideological basis) for the emergence of a new Global Civilization and of a truly World Church. In response, John attempted to confirm, further specific, and add to the principles of Catholic Social Teaching to meet this new global challenge.

Also, for societal life John sought to retain a balanced emphasis on rural life, with the family farm still at its center, and to keep an urban-rural balance across what he hoped would become a more balanced global development. He also further strengthened the Church's commitment to workers articulated in Leo XIII's call for harmony between labor and capital and the call of Pius XI for new forms of worker self-management. And he clearly identified the Church with the newly liberated colonial world and offered strong support for its 'development.'

Interestingly, in ecclesial life, and I believe for the first time in the tradition of papal encyclicals which began in 1740, John no longer

---

[85] Par. 6.

[86] Par. 262.

referred to the laity as *children*. The laity was now elevated to adulthood as his *sons* – a title given formerly in papal encyclicals only to priests. But he did not yet embrace gender-inclusive language (to be fair, hardly anyone did at the time), and his message was still set within the framework of a non-evangelical clerical familial patriarchy.

So the patriarchal interpretation of society, marriage, and family remained. Also, the ecclesiology remained patriarchal, with the pope as *'father,'* the bishops as *'brothers,'* and the laity now joining priests as *'sons.'* (Such a patriarchal interpretation of the Church, of course, is not found in the New Testament.) Coming from John, however, at such an advanced age and expressing such a warm and humble personal style, the harsh edges of patriarchy were inevitably softened into the warm comfort of a loving grandfather.

Finally, and uniquely in this document, John also referred to the entire human race as his *'children.'* His intention was to place the Church not only at the service of the modern industrial West but also at the service of the entire human family and especially in the post-colonial areas. No doubt his loving grandfather-like character again broke through any patriarchal limits to reveal his deep love for all of humanity.

5

LABOREM EXERCENS

"On Human Work"
1981 Encyclical of John Paul II
Written for the 90ᵗʰ Anniversary of Rerum Novarum

Excerpt from an unfinished and unpublished manuscript by Joe Holland
on the social teachings of John Paul II

I n 1981, for the 90ᵗʰ anniversary of Leo XIII's 1891 encyclical RERUM NOVARUM, John Paul II (1978-2005) issued his third encyclical letter, LABOREM EXERCENS, on human work.[1] Delayed by hospitalization following an attempt on his life, the pope promulgated the document on 14 September, rather than on the anniversary date of 15 May. Like his 1979 encyclical REDEMPTOR HOMINIS, this one was addressed to "Brothers in the Episcopate, to the Priests, to the Religious Families, to the Sons and Daughters of the Church, and to all Men and Women of Good Will."[2]

---

[1] The official English version may be found on the website of the Vatican at: *http://www.vatican.va/holy_father/john_paul_ii/encyclicals/documents/hf_jp-ii_enc_14091981_laborem-exercens_en.html* (accessed 2012-05-01).

[2] Curiously, the laity, though now distinguished by gender, is nonetheless described as not part of Church, but rather as external "sons and daughters of the Church." This is not an ecclesiology grounded in the New Testament.

In addition to its wider applications, this document was John Paul's special gift to the workers in the Polish anti-communist workers' union known as *Solidarnösc* (Solidarity). It may also be considered John Paul's most dramatic statement in support of workers and workers' unions.

The document opens with a brief statement of the meaning of human work, be it manual or intellectual, as a vocation rooted in human beings' creation in "the image and likeness of God," because of which, John Paul wrote, humans are called to work at the process of "subduing" Earth – thus distinguishing humanity from the rest of creation. Also, this process of human work is seen as the "mark of a person operating within a community of persons."[3] The document then continues with the following sections:

- *Introduction* - human work described as "the essential key" to "the whole social question;"

- *Nature of Human Work* - the primacy of the "subjective" side of work as first revealed in the Book of Genesis, the destructive inversion of work by the "materialistic economism" called "Capitalism" which has given priority to the "objective" side, and the recovery through "solidarity" of the subjective side in relation to the person, family, and society;

- *Conflict between Labor and Capital* - the historical unfolding of "economism" as the fundamental error concerning work, both as the practical materialism of "rigid Capitalism" and as the "theoretical materialism" of Marxism, to be countered by the principle of *the "priority of labor" in relation to capital;*

---

[3] Par. 1.

- *Priority of labor* – a catalogue of the rights of workers, as flowing from the priority of labor, including unions as a "constructive factor of social order and solidarity;"

- *Spirituality of Work* – in its general human dimension as sharing in body and spirit in the Creator's own creativity by "unfolding the Creator's work" and "contributing ... to the realization of the divine plan," and in its specifically Christian dimension as redeemed by Jesus' own work, as well as by his cross and resurrection.

Introduction
Work as Key to Social Question

While in Redemptor Hominis John Paul had described humanity as "the primary and fundamental way for the church," here he concretized human work as "a perennial and fundamental" aspect of the *human* way. In light of the global and electronic character of contemporary society, he further proposed that attention to the new context of work was important. He claimed that we now stood

> ... *on the eve of new developments in technological, economic and political conditions which, according to many experts, will influence the world of work and production no less than the industrial revolution of the last century.*

He noted the impact of automation, as well as the new realization of ecological threats, plus the political emergence of peoples formerly subjugated. He also pointed out the great dislocation caused by unemployment.[4]

---

4 Pars. 2-4, for this paragraph and the preceding quote and prior paragraph.

In light of this new situation, John Paul called for "the discovery of new meanings of human work." Praising the recent work of the Pontifical Commission Justice and Peace, as well as corresponding bodies within various bishops conferences, he distinguished what he saw as *a new period of Catholic Social Teaching* from its earlier roots.

Thus, he pointed out, from Leo XIII's RERUM NOVARUM to Pius XI's QUADRAGESIMO ANNO, "the church's teaching concentrates mainly on the just solution of the 'labor question' within individual nations." In the new period, which he saw epitomized by John XXIII's MATER ET MAGISTRA, Vatican II's GAUDIUM ET SPES, and Paul VI's POPULORUM PROGRESSIO, the focus shifted to the global relationship among countries.

John Paul described this period of the Church's teaching as widening its horizon to take in "the world." This meant, he wrote, placing particular emphasis on "the disproportionate distribution of wealth and poverty and the existence of some countries and continents that are developed and of others that are not," and calling for "a leveling out and for a search for ways to ensure just development for all."

Thus, for John Paul's analysis, the Leonine period concentrated on the *class* question, while the Johannine period emphasized the international or *global* question. Now, he proposed, he would *link together* the class dimension and the global dimension.[5]

---

[5] Pars. 6-9 for this and the preceding paragraphs. Note that John Paul's intimation that MATER AND MAGISTRA, with its global emphasis, did not do equal justice to the class question of workers, and his statement that he will link the two, do not seem accurate as should be clear from this book's earlier summary of MATER ET MAGIstra. John Paul is thus continuing the global-class linkage already established by John.

John Paul traced the roots of Catholic Social Teaching back to the Book of Genesis and the New Testament. Though these original teachings had been continually "brought up to date," he claimed, their "Christian basis of truth was "ageless." Despite this ageless character, however, he announced that he now wished to highlight a theme "more than had been done before," namely "the fact that human work is a key, probably the essential key, to the whole social question."[6]

Nature of Human Work

According to John Paul, the BOOK OF GENESIS revealed the most fundamental truth about work. *Human work participated in God's own creativity,* for it was rooted in the image of God within humanity, and expressed itself in a specific human "domination ... over the earth," in response to God's mandate for humans to "subdue" the earth.[7] The whole progress of Science and Technology need to be seen, he argued, as the attempted unfolding of this mandate, through such progress was also subject to distortion.

As man, through his work, becomes more and more the master of the earth, and as he confirms his dominion over the visible world,[8]

---

[6] Pars. 10-11.

[7] This insight is indeed a new and powerful development in Catholic Social Teaching, in a Theology of Human Work, and in a Theology of the Laity. The insight was developed earlier by the founder of Opus Dei, Josemaría Escrivá de Balaguer, who was canonized a saint in 2002 by John Paul II (reportedly himself close to Opus Dei). To my knowledge, however, Escrivá never linked this important insight to contemporary Catholic Social Teaching's core theme of the essential role of workers' unions. Indeed, unless I am mistaken, this core theme seems notably absent from Escrivá's Theology of Work.

[8] John Paul's use here of human "domination" or "subduing" of Earth reflects the standard 'Dominion Theology' found in most translations of Genesis 1: 26 & 27. Yet some scholars have suggested that a more accurate translation of the

again through his work, he nevertheless remains in every case and at every phase of this process within the Creator's original ordering.

And this ordering remains necessarily and indissolubly linked with the fact that man was created, as male and female, "in the image of God" ... Each and every individual, to the proper extent and in an incalculable number of ways, takes part in the giant process whereby man "subdues the earth" through his work.[9]

Then John Paul established a theme that would be central to the whole argument of this encyclical, namely his distinction between *the subjective* and *objective* dimensions of human work.

Objective Dimension

The *objective* dimension of work refers to the *products of work*, including the technological tools being used, which were the product of earlier work. The objective side of work has a history of phases, including the phase through which we had just come, and now the new phase marked by the "development of new technologies, such as electronics and the microprocessor," as seen "especially in the fields of miniaturization, communications, and telecommunications."[10]

Technology of itself, John Paul claimed, was "undoubtedly humanity's "ally," since it was an expression of human creativity and

---

Hebrew word *kabash* – in their view wrongly translated as 'domination' – would portray humanity as called to become spiritually one with Earth and to sanctify it. But exploring that important possibility is a task beyond this book

[9] Par. 15 for the quotation, and pars. 12-15 for the full section.

[10] Pars. 16-19.

a means to further realization of the human vocation to work. But Technology could also be put to anti-human purposes.

> *In some instances, Technology can cease to be man's ally and become almost his enemy, as when the mechanization of work "supplants" him, taking away all personal satisfaction and the incentive to creativity and responsibility, when it deprives many workers of their previous employment, or when, through exalting the machine, it reduces man to the status of a slave.*[11]

Whether Technology is functioning in its proper role as an ally of humanity, or whether it has been turned against human purposes, was for John Paul a question of "an ethical and social character," which brings us to the subjective side of human work, namely humanity itself.

Subjective Dimension

For John Paul, work in the *subjective* sense refers to the *human person*, created as the image of God and realizing that image in work: "As a person, man is therefore the subject of work." Regardless of its objective content, work only has meaning, according to John Paul, only in so far as it serves "to realize (one's) humanity." This requires that work as a process be performed in such a way that "the one who carries it out is a person, a conscious and free subject, that is to say, a subject who decides about himself." This, he proposed, "constitutes the fundamental and perennial heart of Christian teaching on human work," and has "primary significance for the formulation of the important social problems characterizing whole ages."[12]

---

[11] Par. 19.

[12] Pars. 22-25.

In the "ancient world," John Paul noted, people were divided into "classes" according to their work, and often "free men" were immune from the obligation of physical work, which was then given to "slaves." He noted that, while initially Christianity did not condemn slavery, it did nonetheless transform its subjective meaning, so that manual workers and even slaves came to be considered as having equal dignity with "free men."

Thus, just as Jesus worked at the carpenter's bench, so all humans need to be seen as gathered in the equal of dignity of persons around the workbench of life. "The primary sources of the dignity of work," therefore, are to found "primarily in the subjective dimension, not in the objective one." "Such a concept," he claimed, "practically does away with the very basis of the ancient differentiation of people into classes (e.g., free persons and slaves) according to the kind of work done".[13]

Conflict between Labor and Capital

In a similar manner, since beginning of "the industrial age" in "the modern period," John Paul maintained, the church had to struggle against defining workers only by the objective dimension of work.

He described the modern error as "various trends of *materialistic* and *economistic* thought" (italics added). By "materialistic and economistic thought," he meant that the worker was defined only in terms of the objective dimension of work, *with the person of the worker seen only as an instrument* in larger objective economic processes.[14]

---

[13] Pars. 25-27 for this and the prior paragraph above.

[14] Par. 28.

Materialist Error of Labor as Commodity

The first expression of this materialist and economistic error, appearing in the nineteenth century, was the modern liberal (capitalist) doctrine that labor was a *commodity* or "merchandise" to be bought and sold on the free market like any other resource or product.

Later, he said, this error was mitigated by "the development of various forms of Capitalism – parallel with various forms of collectivism." These developments included "the activity of workers' associations and public authorities." But, he proposed, the danger of treating work as an objective force (as in 'workforce') still persisted, particularly as the discipline of economics was still "marked by the premises of materialistic economism."[15]

The result of this economism, according to John Paul, was "development of a *one-sided materialistic civilization, which gives prime importance to the objective dimension of work*, while the subjective dimension ... remains on a secondary level" (italics added). This result, he argued, represented "confusion or even a reversal of the order laid down from the beginning by the words of the Book of Genesis."

To this reversal, John Paul gave the overarching name of "Capitalism," a generic name that in this section covered even socialist variants.

> *Man is treated as an instrument of production, whereas he – alone, independent of the work he does – ought to be treated as the effective subject of work and its true maker and creator. Precisely this reversal of order, whatever the program or name under which*

---

[15] Par. 29.

it occurs, should rightly be called "Capitalism" – in the sense explained below. Everybody knows that Capitalism has a definite historical meaning as a system, an economic and social system, opposed to "Socialism" or "Communism."

But, in light of the analysis of the fundamental reality of the whole economic process – first and foremost of the production structure that work is – it should be recognized that the error of early Capitalism can be repeated when ever man is in a way treated on the same level as the whole complex of the material means of production, as an instrument and not in accordance with the true dignity of his work – that is to say, where he is not treated as subject and maker, and for this very reason as the true purpose of the whole process of production.[16]

Response of Worker Solidarity

During the last century, John Paul recalled, the injustices of Capitalism "gave rise to a just social reaction and caused the impetuous emergence of a great burst of solidarity among workers, first and foremost industrial workers.[17] In such situations where "the machine tends to dominate man," "the call to solidarity" represented something "important and eloquent from the view of social ethics."

It was the reaction against the degradation of man as the subject of work and against the unheard-of accompanying exploitation in the field of wages, working conditions and social security for the

---

[16] Par. 30.

[17] Par. 32.

worker. This reaction united the working world in a community marked by great solidarity.[18]

The root of the problem, according to John Paul, was again the economistic assumptions of the liberal (capitalist) ideology:

This state of affairs was favored by the liberal socio-political system which in accordance with its "economistic" premises, strengthened and safeguarded economic initiative by the possessors of capital alone, but did not pay sufficient attention to the rights of the workers, on the grounds that human work is solely an instrument of production, and that capital is the basis, efficient factor and purpose of production.[19]

In the wake of the social reaction against this error, John Paul recalled, there emerged a broad "worker solidarity" plus profound changes in society, leading to new and different "forms of neo-Capitalism or collectivism." In addition, various systems were developed for workers to "share in running businesses and in controlling their productivity," and workers began to do this in part through the influence their "associations" exercise "over conditions of work and pay, and also over social legislation."[20]

Need for Global Solidarity

But, for John Paul, with the development of global communications and a new global civilization, this error of early Capitalism revealed "other forms of injustice much more extensive than those (of) the last century." Further, a "proletarian situation" was being

---

[18] Par. 33.

[19] Par. 34.

[20] Par. 35.

extended even to "intellectuals" in their work and in the broad "unemployment of intellectuals. Hence there was need for a still broader solidarity on a global scale: solidarity both on behalf of workers and against poverty and hunger. Seeking to support this world solidarity, the church could truly be called a *"church of the poor"* (italics added).[21]

According to John Paul, this new and broader solidarity, rooted in the mystery of the human person, needed to promote a profound sense of the dignity and goodness of human work, and in turn to be extended to agricultural workers, industrial workers, intellectual workers, and service workers across the planet. It also needed to commend "the virtue of industriousness," even while condemning various ways that work has been used "against man," for example, in "the system of forced labor in concentration camps."

Further, the foundation dignity of human work with its roots in the person should be extended to the "secondary sphere" of the family. For family is "a community made possible by work and the first school of work," and to the "tertiary sphere" of "the great society," which represents "a great historical and social incarnation of the work of all generations." In all three spheres, he argued, it must be the subjective dimension of work, realized as "dominion over the world of nature," that remains primary.[22]

Priority of Labor over Capital

John Paul praised the many attempts to re-establish and to defend the subjective dimension of labor. In particular, he mentioned work on behalf of *human rights*, which included *labor rights*, and

---

[21] Pars. 35-37.

[22] Pars. 38-45.

especially the work of "the International Labor Organization, the oldest specialized agency of the United Nations." (As noted earlier, it preceded the UN.) He also pointed out that the conflict between labor and capital had been transformed into an "ideological conflict between Liberalism, understood as the ideology of Capitalism, and Marxism, understood as the ideology of Scientific Socialism and Communism."[23]

Capital and Labor

In particular, John Paul lamented, the *real conflict between capital and labor*, which was also a *conflict between the objective and subjective dimensions of work*, was unfortunately transformed into "a systematic class struggle conducted not only by ideological means, but also and chiefly by political means." Under "the philosophy of Marx and Engels," this led to "collectivization of the means of production" and "the dictatorship of the proletariat."[24]

The *solution to both the liberal (capitalist) and socialist errors*, according to John Paul, was to "go back to the fundamental issue of human work," and there to reassert the subjective dimension of labor. Or, as he put it, to "first of all recall a principle that has always been taught by the church: **the principle of the priority of labor over capital**" (bold added).[25]

---

23 Pars. 46-49.

24 Par. 49.

25 Par. 51-52. As Michael Schuck has noted, though John Paul claimed that the church had always taught the principle of "the priority of labor over capital," there was no prior *explicit* mention of this phrase in the entire corpus of papal encyclicals. See Schuck, THAT THEY BE ONE: THE SOCIAL TEACHING OF THE PAPAL ENCYCLICALS 1740-1989 (Georgetown University Press, 1991) p. 169, n. 94.

John Paul here used the term "capital" in a way different from its earlier use in the tradition of papal social teaching. From Leo XIII forward, capital meant the capitalist class, and the proposed harmony between capital and labor was to be a harmony between employee and employer.

Presumably because, in his earlier role as Professor of Social Ethics in communist Poland, his own readings in Economics had including texts from the Marxian tradition, John Paul used the term capital to refer to "the means of production," both natural and technological. This was the definition established by Karl Marx to describe nature and reified past labor as the *objective* forces of capital. Thus John Paul wrote:

> Since the concept of capital includes not only the natural resources placed at man's disposal, but also the whole collection of means by which man appropriates natural resources and transforms them in accordance with his needs (and thus in a sense humanizes them), it must immediately be noted that all these means are the result of the historical heritage of human labor.
>
> All the means of production, from the most primitive to the ultramodern one – it is man that has gradually developed them ... This gigantic and powerful instrument – the whole collection of means of production that in a sense are considered synonymous with "capital" – is the result of work and bears the signs of human labor.[26]

Again, such language clearly reflects the insights of Marx regarding what he called the "means of production."

---

[26] Pars. 55-56.

Over against this reification of labor into capital and its subsequent domination over workers, John Paul insisted on "the primacy of man over things." In his view, "Everything contained in the concept of capital in the strict sense is only a collection of things."[27]

Yet, John Paul maintained, labor and capital were not opposed, for they represented nothing more than the "workers" and the "workbench." Provided priority was given to the worker, how could the workbench be opposed to the worker? If the subject were truly given priority, the object would be the instrument of the subject and not its enemy.[28]

Economism as Root Error

The antagonism of capital against labor, John Paul again argued, was rooted in the modern error of *economism*. This error considered "human labor solely according to its economic purpose." Fundamentally, this was an error of "materialism" – not initially of a *socialist* "theoretical materialism" but rather of a *capitalist* "practical materialism," that is,

> .... a materialism judged capable of satisfying man's needs not so much on the grounds of premises derived from materialist theory as on the grounds of a particular way of evaluating things and so on the grounds of a certain hierarchy of goods based on the greater immediate attractiveness of what is material.[29]

Further, according to John Paul, this "practical materialism" went "hand in hand with the formation of a *materialist philosophy*" (ital-

---

[27] Par. 57.

[28] Pars. 58-60.

[29] Par. 60.

ics added), a kind of "common materialism" which professed "to reduce spiritual reality to a superfluous phenomenon." Only later, he wrote, did it develop into the Marxian philosophy called "dialectical materialism." Yet it was not Marxism, but rather "this (capitalist) practical error" which "struck a blow first and foremost against human labor."

He continued to argue that this "same error," originally connected with "the period of primitive Capitalism," was repeated whenever "people's thinking" began with "the same theoretical or practical premises." Now, he claimed, this same error was spreading to the relations among nations.[30]

Property and Socialization

John Paul also addressed the theme of the ownership of private property, and he linked this theme to the relationship of workers and entrepreneurs. He noted that, against Marxian collectivism, the Church had traditionally defended the right of private property, including the right to ownership of productive property.

He also recalled the traditional Catholic teaching that this right to ownership was not an absolute right, but rather a limited right set within the more "broader context of the right common to all to use the goods of the whole creation." He insisted that "the right to private property" was "subordinated to the right to common use, to the fact that goods are meant for everyone."[31]

Further, he argued that the Catholic tradition had never understood ownership "in a way that could constitute grounds for social

---

[30] Pars. 60-63.

[31] Pars. 63-64.

conflict in labor, and that this especially applied to "ownership of the means of production." The reason for this, he continued, was that "the only legitimate title" to possession of "the means of production," whether as privately or publicly owned, was

> ... that they should serve labor and thus by serving labor that they should make possible the achievement of the first principle of this order, namely the universal destination of goods and the right to common use of them.[32]

For this reason, John Paul continued, "one cannot exclude the *socialization* (italics added), in suitable conditions, of certain means of production."[33] He then again repeated his judgment that "the position of 'rigid' Capitalism continued to remain unacceptable, namely the position that defended the exclusive right to private ownership of the means of production as an untouchable 'dogma' of economic life."

Logically, therefore, he commended "the many proposals put forth by experts in Catholic Social Teaching and by the highest magisterium of the church" – for example, "proposals for joint ownership of the means of work, sharing by the workers in the management and-or profits of business, so-called share-holding by labor, etc." Whether or not these particular proposal were feasible in concrete circumstances, he insisted that "recognition of the proper position of labor and the worker in the production process

---

[32] Par. 65.

[33] Recall that the term *socialization* was first introduced into Catholic Social Teaching by John XXIII in MATER ET MAGISTRA. Here John Paul confirms it. When the term first appeared in John XXIII's encyclical, the late William F. Buckley's NATIONAL REVIEW – boldly rejecting the Church's social magisterium – responded with the slogan *"Mater si, magistra no."*
See: http://en.wikipedia.org/wiki/Mater_si,_magistra_no (accessed 2012-05-01).

demanded various adaptations in the sphere of the right to owner-ship of the means of production," and particularly in the Third World.[34]

"Therefore," John Paul concluded, "the position of 'rigid' Capital-ism must undergo continual revision," but not to the extreme of "an *a priori* elimination of private ownership of the means of pro-duction." He warned that "merely converting the means of pro-duction into state property in the collectivist system is by no means equivalent to 'socializing' that property." For such collecti-vization can create a new "monopoly of administration" under-mining basic human rights.

Such collectivization of property, he argued, would simply trans-fer it from the control by a *private elite* to control by a *public elite,* and not truly return control to the workers.

Rather he encouraged "associating labor with the ownership of capital, as far as possible," and "producing a wide range of inter-mediate bodies ... enjoying real autonomy with regard to the pub-lic powers." Otherwise the worker would feel like "just a cog in a huge machine moved from above."[35]

Rights of Workers

John Paul next examined the rights and duties of workers, as de-rived from his personalist and solidarity view of human labor. These included the following.

- *Work as a Human Obligation.* Work is a human duty com-manded by God, because it is a key way for humans to fulfill

---

[34] Par. 66-67.

[35] Par. 68-71.

themselves, as well as to serve others. It includes the task of carrying on the work of past generations to which current workers are heir, and also the task of sharing in building the future for new generations.[36]

- *The Indirect Employer.* The "indirect employer" includes "both persons and institutions of various kinds, and also collective labor contracts and the principles of conduct which are laid down by these persons and institutions and which determine the whole socioeconomic system or are its result." "All these influences must be kept in mind" when "establishing an ethically correct labor policy.[37]

- *Rich and Poor Countries.* The state, a key instance of the indirect employer "must conduct a just labor policy," particularly in trade policies between rich and poor countries.[38]

- *Criterion of Maximum Profit.* The network of persons, policies, and institutions called the indirect employer must never leave workers rights to "merely the result of economic systems which on a larger or smaller scale are guided chiefly by the criterion of maximum profit." To the contrary, "respect for the fundamental rights of the worker" must "constitute the adequate and fundamental criterion for shaping the whole economy, both on the level of individual society and state and within the whole of the world economic policy." Special mention is made of international organizations, particularly the UN's In-

---

[36] Pars. 72-73.

[37] Par. 77.

[38] Pars. 78-79.

ternational Labor Organization (ILO) and its Food and Agricultural Organization (FAO).[39]

- **Unemployment.** It is the duty of the indirect employer to create an environment providing "suitable employment for all who are capable of it." In contemporary times, this means especially for the young, as well as providing unemployment benefits and an "overall planning" to organize work "in a correct and rational way."[40]

- **Economic Planning.** This obligation of planning falls especially on the state, but not as a "one-sided centralization." Rather it is a matter of "coordination" which works with individuals, free groups and local work centers. This planning must also extend to "international collaboration by means of the necessary treaties and agreements," as called for in POPULORUM PROGRESSIO. Such planning must also include the right sectoral balance between agriculture, industry, and services, as well as scientific and artistic work.[41]

- **Just Wage.** In addition to these responsibilities of the indirect employer, the direct employer in the immediate relationship with the worker has the obligation of paying "a just remuneration for work done." This just wage needs to be determined in light of "the principle of the common use of goods," as well as the needs of the family. The family's needs can be met either

---

[39] Pars. 80-81.

[40] Pars. 82-83.

[41] Pars. 83-86.

by a "family wage," or by other social measures, such as "allowances or grants to mothers."[42]

- *Mothers' Role.* It is wrong to structure the labor process in a way which penalizes mothers and their care of children. For a mother to have to abandon her children to take up work outside of home injures the society and the family. "The true advancement of women requires that labor should be structured in such a way that women do not have to pay for their advancement by abandoning what is specific to them and at the expense of the family, in which women as mothers have an irreplaceable role."[43]

- *Rights of Workers.* Other social benefits, which should be provided for workers, include: health-care, and particularly for accidents at work; the right to rest at least on Sunday and also for holidays and/or a vacation; the right to a pension and insurance for old age and also for accidents in work; and the right to a physically and morally safe working environment.[44]

- *Right of Association.* Workers have the right "to form associations," called labor or trade unions, in order to defend their interests. Such organizations are *"an indispensable element of social life"* (italics added), and could be organized in any profession or area of work.

The struggle of unions, however, is not against other persons, but for the just good. Such struggle does not ultimately seek

---

[42] Pars. 88-90.

[43] Pars. 91-92. (Note that at this point there is no reference to a father's role in caring for children, even though paradoxically John Paul was mostly raised by his father, since his mother died when he was very young.)

[44] Par. 93.

"to eliminate the opponent," but rather "to build up a community." While unions remain "a constructive factor of social order and solidarity," their "demands" should not be "turned into a kind of group or class egoism." Neither should unions have the character of a political party, nor be subject to a political party. The strike, though it should not be abused, is a real right to be exercised in extreme cases, though not against the common good of the whole society.[45]

- *Agricultural Work.* Agriculture is of fundamental importance for society, and agricultural workers need to have their rights recognized. In many cases there is an urgent need "to restore to agriculture – and to rural people – its just value as the basis for a healthy economy."[46]

- *Disabled Persons.* Disabled persons have the same rights to work and as workers as other persons, and they "should be helped to participate in the life of society in all its aspects and at all the levels accessible to their capacities." Further, it is wrong to practice a discrimination "of the strong and healthy against the weak and sick." Finally, such persons should be provided with "professional training and work," as well as supportive "physical and psychological working conditions."[47]

- *Migrant Workers.* Migration, while tragic, is in many cases "a necessary evil," but it does not thereby rob migrating workers of their rights as persons. In addition, society has an obligation to reduce where possible the harmful impact of immigration

---

[45] Pars. 94-100.

[46] Pars. 101-103.

[47] Pars. 104-106.

by just legislation. In particular, such workers should never be taken advantage of because of their precarious status.[48]

Spirituality of Work

John Paul concluded this landmark encyclical with reflections on the spirituality of work. He pointed out that work always involved "the whole person, body and spirit." The heart of this spirituality, already developed earlier in the text, is that "man, created in God's image, received a mandate to subject to himself the earth and all that it contains, and to govern the world with justice and holiness." John Paul described the spirituality of work as workers' subjective awareness of being *co-creators* with the Creator.[49]

The first "gospel of work" to celebrate this doctrine, according to John Paul, was the BOOK OF GENESIS. Later, he wrote, Jesus revealed the redemptive and the creative dimension of the spirituality of work. Workers truly "by their labor" are "unfolding the Creator's work, consulting the advantages of their brothers and sisters, and contributing by their personal industry to the realization in history of the divine plan."

In this process, workers need to "learn the deepest meaning and the value of all creation, and its orientation to the praise of God." They do this by achieving "competence in secular fields and by their personal activity." Thus, "by means of work (humanity) participates in the activity of God." Even manual work, John Paul maintained, was celebrated by Jesus the carpenter, who in turn

---

[48] Pars. 107-110.

[49] Pars. 110-113.

described his Father as a "vinedresser," a manual worker. The apostle Paul also boasted of his trade, apparently a tentmaker.[50]

Yet, despite the "original blessing" of its goodness and even its divine vocation, he noted that work nonetheless carried the effects of sin, and so was experienced as the "curse" of "toil." This toil in turn "constituted an announcement of death." But Jesus took up this curse and redeemed it in the paschal mystery. So too workers share in this paschal mystery through the suffering of their own work, as they struggle to bring for a "new earth" where "justice dwells." While ultimately "the growth of Christ's Kingdom" can never be reduced to "earthly progress, nonetheless "the better ordering of human society ... is of vital concern to the kingdom of God."[51]

John Paul ended this encyclical by noting that "it is through (human) labor that not only 'the fruits of our activity,' but also 'human dignity, brotherhood and freedom' must increase on earth."[52]

This document, like the general corpus of John Paul's work, emphasized the principles of *divine and human transcendence*, with human transcendence described as a *masculine domination* over nature.

From the perspective of more recent developments in feminine and ecological thought, current and future contributors to Catholic Social Teaching will presumably also emphasize the celebration of *feminine* modes of participation in divine creativity, as well as God's inseparable *transcendent-and-immanent* presence within crea-

---

[50] Pars. 114-122.

[51] Pars. 125-130.

[52] Par. 131.

tion, and nature's own immanent evolutionary-creative participation in divine creativity, along with humanity's holistic participation in the creative matrix of *nature' creativity*, all of which flow from the ultimate creativity of the Creator.

Nonetheless, John Paul's powerful emphasis on human creativity within work, in turn spiritually communing with God's own creativity, represents, I propose, the most powerful new development in Catholic Social Teaching since RERUM NOVARUM.

6

CENTESIMUS ANNUS

"The Hundredth Year"
Written for the 100ᵗʰ Anniversary of Rerum Novarum
1991 Encyclical of John Paul II

An excerpt from an unfinished manuscript by Joe Holland
on the Social Teachings of John Paul II

I n May of 1991, on the 100ᵗʰ anniversary of RERUM NOVARUM, John Paul II issued his ninth encyclical, CENTESIMUS ANNUS.[1] The document was addressed to "Brothers in the Episcopate, Priests and Deacons, Families of Men and Women Religious, All the Christian Faithful, and All Men and Women of Good Will," with all but bishops greeted as "Sons and Daughters." Noteworthy was the acknowledgment of "Deacons," as well as the explicit mention of "Women" for the religious families.

---

[1] The official English translation may be found on the website of the Vatican at: *http://www.vatican.va/holy_father/john_paul_ii/encyclicals/documents/hf_jp-ii_enc_01051991_centesimus-annus_en.html* (accessed 2012-05-01).

While the anniversary of RERUM NOVARUM was the main reason for the document, its writing was dramatically marked by another historic event, namely the liberation of Eastern Europe due to the fall of Soviet Communism during late 1989 and early 1990.[2] These two reasons for writing the document were not separate. RERUM NOVARUM had been among the first papal encyclicals aimed at combating Socialism. Now, one hundred years later, this document celebrated the defeat of Soviet Communism.

In this encyclical, John Paul described his task as "a 're-reading' of Pope Leo's encyclical" first by "looking back" (to the past), second by "looking around" (to the present), and third by "looking (ahead) to the future." In particular, facing the dawn of the third millennium of Christianity, he wrote of "uncertainties and promises which appeal to our imagination and creativity." He also wrote of the "the responsibility of pastors to give careful consideration to current events in order to discern the new requirements of evangelization."[3]

After a brief Introduction, the encyclical was divided into six sections titled as follows:

- The Contributions of Leo's Encyclical
- The 'New Things' of Today
- The Year 1989
- Private Property and Universal Destination of Material Goods
- The State and Culture
- Humanity as the Way of the Church

---

[2] There is a whole section on these events, and they in turn color the entire document. See especially pars. 29.

[3] Par. 3.

Yet, in the imaginative style found elsewhere in his writings, John Paul was not constrained by the linear logic of his outline. Consequently, various themes specific to one section regularly appear in other sections as well.

The entire encyclical is grounded on John Paul's foundational theme of *Christian personalism*, that is, the transcendent dignity of the human person as created in the image of God. Also, this document provided significant endorsements to the validity and importance of the free market and what he called not Capitalism but the *"business economy"* (italics added), though still with all the qualifications of his earlier encyclical on human labor and of Catholic Social Teaching generally.

Contributions of Leo's Encyclical

In the first section, John Paul, using the perspective of his favorite theme, offered a review of the significance of RERUM NOVARUM at the time it was issued. Accordingly, he viewed the "guiding principle" of the encyclical as Christian personalism: "a correct view of the human person and of his unique value (as) ... the only creature on earth which God willed for itself."[4]

He also saw all the evils to which RERUM NOVARUM responded as having their origin in the divorce between economic and social "freedom" and the "truth about man." Further, he saw this foundational document of the church's modern social teaching as achieving for the church the status of a "public citizenship," which then enabled it to speak forcefully as a participant in society. In addition, he saw this social teaching as inextricably linked to evangelization, and to the Christian message about the dignity of

---

[4] Par. 11.

the worker and the dignity of work as a human vocation embedded within a social dimension.[5]

John Paul noted that Leo's "new things" included a new form of ownership, that is, of "capital" and not simply of land, and also of a new form of labor, that is, "wage labor" – wrongly treated by the owners of capital as if it were only a commodity. He also noted that the "prevailing political theory" wrongly denied the state any legal interventionist responsibility for the common good. And he praised Leo for seeing early on the "danger of a revolution fanned by ideals that were then called 'socialist'."[6]

John Paul further praised Leo for supporting the right of "trade unions" to organize and to demand legitimate labor rights, which included "limitation of working hours" and a "just wage," and in general to attempt to restrain "unbridled Capitalism." He saw in Leo's insistence on the workers' right to perform their religious duties "a springboard for the principle of religious freedom."

Overall he interpreted Leo's response as guided by "the principle of solidarity," which, he stated, Leo had called "friendship," which Pius XI had called "social charity," and which Paul VI had called "a civilization of love." In addition, he saw Leo's encyclical as a powerful expression of the church's perennial *"preferential option for the poor"*(italics added). But he also noted that, while Leo called for state intervention on behalf of the workers, he also "frequently (insisted) on necessary limits to the state's intervention and on its instrumental character."[7]

---

[5] Pars. 4-6.

[6] Pars. 4-5.

[7] Pars. 7-11.

New Things of Today

John Paul opened his second section of this encyclical with a reference to "the events which took place near the end of 1989 and at
the beginning of 1990" (the fall of Soviet Communism, which
would be the subject of his next section).[8] This led him into an extended three-fold analysis:

- First, of why Socialism had failed
- Second, of the wider consequences, from World War I through
  World War II, of the cultural error of the Modern European Enlightenment
- Third, of the post World War II experience, seen as marked by
  great social problems but also by attempts to build democratic
  and just societies

Why Socialism Failed

First, John Paul addressed the failure of Socialism. He ascribed this
failure to a "fundamental error" which was "anthropological in
nature." Referring to the modern European Enlightenment's ap-
propriation of the *mechanistic* cosmology from Newtonian Physics
(and Cartesian Philosophy) for the philosophical explanation of
society, he stated that this "fundamental error" was to consider
the human person as "simply an element, a *molecule* (italics added)
within the social organism" and "without reference to his free
choice."[9]

---

[8] Par. 12.

[9] On the Enlightenment's mechanistic root-metaphor (the social application of
the modern atomistic-mechanistic Cartesian-Newtonian Cosmology), and on
social metaphors in general, see my essay, "Linking Social Analysis and Theological Reflection: The Place of Root Metaphors in Social and Religious Reflec-

Returning to his personalist theme, the pope claimed that in this *mechanistic* view "the concept of the person as the autonomous subject of moral decision disappears," and also that, having denied this subjective dimension, so too there followed logically a denial of the right of private property. As a result, he continued, society appeared only as a "social *machine*" (italics added), without "authentic human community." Such a state reduced "every citizen to being a 'cog' in the state *machinery*" (italics added)[10]

In contrast to this error, John Paul held up "the Christian vision of the human person" as grounding "a correct picture of society." In this vision, he argued, "the social nature of man is not completely fulfilled in the state, but is realized in various intermediate groups." Following his analysis of work in LABOREM EXERCENS, he called this extra-political role "the 'subjectivity' of society," which, "together with the subjectivity of the individual, was canceled out by 'Real Socialism'."

The still deeper root of this fundamentally erroneous error, according to John Paul, was *atheism*. It was in "the denial of God" that the human person was first deprived "of his foundation." Thus, for this analysis, *without God there was no transcendence*, without transcendence there was *no person*, and without the person there was *no authentic freedom or real community*. He saw atheism as "closely connected with the Enlightenment" and with its "mechanistic way" of viewing the "human and social reality."[11]

---

tion," in James E. Hug, SJ, TRACING THE SPIRIT: COMMUNITIES, SOCIAL ACTION, AND THEOLOGICAL REFLECTION (New York: Paulist Press, 1983).

[10] Pars. 12-13 & 15.

[11] Par. 13.

A major consequence of this *mechanistic* anthropology, John Paul continued, was "class struggle." It is important, however, to distinguish what he meant here by this phrase, for in his lexicon it had a limited and still interesting significance. For him, class struggle was something different from the general "struggle for justice," which his beloved Polish labor union, *Solidarnösc,* had so obviously conducted.

Thus he wrote:

> *The pope (he often referred to himself in the third person) does not, of course, intend to condemn every possible form of social conflict. The church is well aware that in course of history conflicts of interest between different social groups inevitably arise, and that in the face of such conflicts Christians must often take a position, honestly and decisively.*

> *The encyclical LABOREM EXERCENS moreover clearly recognized the positive role of conflict when it takes the form of a "struggle for social justice;" QUADRAGESIMO ANNO had already stated that "if the class struggle abstains from enmities and mutual hatred, it gradually changes into an honest discussion of differences founded on a desire for justice."*[12]

"Class struggle" for John Paul thus meant only those struggles between classes which were overwhelmed by hatred, considered not subject to ethics, not open to compromise, and opposed to the common good. He thus defined the phrase narrowly, and did not reject certain other forms of class conflict and the social struggle for authentic justice in which one class does not seek to destroy the other but rather seeks the common good.

---

[12] Par. 14; QUADRAGESIMO ANNO, III:13.

What is condemned in class struggle is the idea that conflict is not restrained by ethical or juridical considerations, or by respect for the dignity of others (and consequently of oneself); a reasonable compromise is thus excluded, and what is pursued is not the general good of society, but a partisan interest which replaces the common good and sets out to destroy whatever stands in its way.[13]

Then John Paul linked "class struggle" within a particular society to "total war" between societies. He saw both Marxism and militarism as two sides of the same coin of Enlightenment *mechanism*, with both guided only by a mechanistic force-field analysis and aiming only at total domination of its own goals.

In a word, it is a question of transferring to the sphere of internal conflict between social groups the doctrine of "total war," which the militarism and imperialism of that time brought to bear on international relations. As a result of this doctrine, the search for a proper balance between the interests of different nations was replaced by attempts to impose the absolute domination of one's own side through the destruction of the other side's capacity to resist, using every possible means, not excluding the use of lies, terror tactics against citizens, and weapons of utter destruction (which precisely in those years were beginning to be designed). Therefore class struggle in the Marxist sense and militarism have the same root, namely atheism and contempt for the human person, which place the principle of force above that of reason and law.[14]

---

[13] Par. 14.

[14] Par. 14. In no way discounting the horrendous atrocities of Soviet Communism, especially under Josef Stalin, it nonetheless seems a questionable reading

In contrast to the totalitarian state, John Paul argued that the correct form of the state would cooperate with associations in society, both directly and indirectly, to establish a "juridical framework" in which the free market might flourish. This would include working for a "certain equality" between parties negotiating within the market system, protecting workers from "the nightmare of unemployment," and ensuring "wage levels adequate for the maintenance of the worker and his family."

---

of the long history of human violence to suggest that the placing of "the principle of force above that of reason and law" has its origin in atheism, and for the modern era in Marxism. Perhaps John Paul's parenthetical comment about the technological power of modern weapons of war might be a more central explanation for the modern "total" warfare – as in the case the atomic bombing of Hiroshima and Nagasaki by a nation made up largely of Christians.

Across human history military leaders, and even religious ones, seemed often quite willing to place "the principle of force above that of reason," though in pre-industrial times they lacked the technological power to inflict the catastrophic damage caused by modern weaponry. Hatred, lies, and terror are hardly unique to the modern post-Enlightenment period.

Indeed, even the biblical mandate of the "ban," described in the dramatic narrative of the original Hebrew conquest of the Canaanite cities, required "total war," namely the "slaughter" of "every man, woman, and child" who lived in those cities. While its historical accuracy may be open to question, the Book of Joshua rejoices that in the cities of Jericho, Ai, Gibeon, Gilgal, Makkedah, Libnah, Lachisch, Eglon, Hebron, and Debir, and "from Kadesh-barnea to Gaza, and "from Goshen to Gibeon," Joshua "left no survivors, but fulfilled the doom on all who lived there" – again, the "slaughter" of every man, woman, and child. (THE BOOK OF JOSHUA, Chapters 1-12.)

Joshua and his army were hardly atheists. Further, this "very great slaughter" would later inspire many Christian-inspired slaughters who also inflicted "total war" in the name of Christian imperialism. So, whatever its historical accuracy, the biblical narrative of Joshua's "very great slaughter" would certainly fulfill the criteria for "total war," as would many later Christian imperialist atrocities.

John Paul placed special emphasis on the role of labor unions within the societal associations. He also described the indirect role of the state as guided by the principle of subsidiarity, and its direct role by solidarity, and especially solidarity with the weakest.

Errors of Enlightenment Seen in Total War

Second, as a preface to his analysis of the wider consequences of the error of the modern European Enlightenment in modern warfare, John Paul summarized his critique of the foundational error regarding the human person, though this time he did not limit the critique to Socialism.

> *This error consists in an understanding of human freedom which detaches it from obedience to the truth, and consequently from the duty to respect the rights of others. The essence of freedom then becomes self-love carried to the point of contempt for God and neighbor, a self-love which leads to an unbridled affirmation of* **self-interest** *and which refuses to be limited by any demand of justice (bold added).*[15]

The mention of "self-interest" cannot be anything but a clear reference to the foundational social principle of Capitalism.

According to John Paul, this error had "extreme consequences in the devastating series of wars which ravaged Europe between 1914 and 1945." He saw these wars as coming from many sources: militarism, exaggerated nationalism, totalitarianism, class struggle, civil strife, or ideological struggle. He singled out in particular the attempted extermination of the Jewish people, "whose terrible

---

[15] Par. 17.

fate has become a symbol of the aberration of which man is capable when he turns against God."[16]

Post World War II Period

Third, John Paul offered both a negative and a positive analysis of the post World War II period up to the present. On the *negative* side, he pointed out that "half the (European) continent fell under the domination of a communist dictatorship, while the other half organized in defense against this threat."

In addition, "an insane arms race swallowed up the resources needed for the development of national economies and for assistance to the less developed nations." In this process, "enormous

---

[16] Par. 17. One might raise a another question here about John Paul's analysis, if we assume that his argument here is a continuation of his immediately prior argument against atheism. Was the Holocaust of the Jews and of the others who died with them in the concentration camps the work of atheists? That would seem a difficult argument to uphold, since Fascism often claimed to be combating 'atheistic Communism' and defending 'Christian Civilization.' Were not many participants in Fascism in fact active Christians, even active Catholic Christian leaders?

Fascism arose to a large degree in Christian cultures like Germany, Italy, and Spain. Indeed, as reported in my earlier book MODERN CATHOLIC SOCIAL TEACHING, many European Catholic leaders saw Fascism as a religious antidote to atheistic Communism, and initially supported it. Further, at least in the beginning, Italian Fascism received significant approval from important Catholic leaders within the Vatican. Indeed, the very creation of the Vatican City-State was the result of a 1929 treaty by the Holy See with the Fascist government of Benito Mussolini. Earlier, many Catholic leaders in the Vatican had apparently provided support for Mussolini's rise to power, with the hope of resolving the 'Roman Question.'

For these reasons, the following new question could be asked: *might there also have been tragic and deep-rooted weaknesses in the modern European Christian evangelization itself, since its history supported so much violence, and since so many of its European leaders seemed at least initially willing to ally themselves with Fascism?*

bloodshed in various parts of the world" occurred on behalf of "the logic of power blocs or empires." "Extremist groups ... were equipped and trained for war," and "many Third World countries" were militarized and led into "fratricidal conflicts." And most menacingly, "atomic war" threatened "suicide of humanity."

All this, according to John Paul, was the result of the Enlightenment's unrestrained *mechanistic* concept of freedom, now institutionalized as "total war" and "class struggle."[17]

On the *positive* side, John Paul saw "in some countries ... a positive effort to rebuild a democratic society inspired by social justice." The purpose of this effort, he proposed, was "to deprive Communism of the revolutionary potential represented by the masses of people subjected to exploitation and oppression." He praised these attempts both for trying "to preserve free market mechanisms," and for avoiding "making market mechanisms the only point of reference for social life." This latter task occurred, he stated, by subjecting the market *mechanisms* "to public control which upholds the principle of the common destination of material goods.[18]

But John Paul saw a *negative* sign in the "setting up of systems of "national security'" to "oppose Marxism." Such systems," he declared, so increased the power of the state as to "run the grave risk

---

[17] Again, though the encyclical laments the Holocaust of the Jews, it seems surprising that, along with the bold and legitimate condemnations of Communism, there is *no explicit reflection on Fascism*, with which so many Catholic Christians, including leaders, seemed to have been complicit. In at least some interpretations, Fascism is an extreme right-wing form of Capitalism, much as Communism is an extreme left-wing form of Socialism. Surely, both extremes deserve close scrutiny by Catholic Social Teaching.

[18] Par. 19.

of destroying the freedom and values of the person, the very things for whose sake it is necessary to oppose Communism."

As with the Leonine popes of the prior strategic stage, John Paul judged dictatorships of the right and those of the left differently. He denounced communist dictatorships on the left for destroying freedom, while he spoke of "national security" dictatorships on the right (in the view of many, *fascist* governments) as running "the risk of destroying freedom."[19]

Another *negative* sign was the emergence of "the affluent society or the consumer society" (primarily in the First World of North America and Western Europe). While the *consumer society* attempted to defeat Marxism by "showing how a free-market society can achieve a greater satisfaction of material values," it also excluded "spiritual values," John Paul argued, and denied "an autonomous existence and value to morality, law, culture and religion." That meant that this society "agreed with Marxism, in the sense that it reduces man to the sphere of economics."[20]

Again on the *positive* side, John Paul praised the post World War II process of *decolonization*. He noted, however, that genuine independence was constrained by the power of "large foreign companies" with only short-term interests in the host country, as well as by the political influence of foreign powers, by unintegrated tribalisms, and by lack of an adequate internal professional class. In such situations, he lamented, many saw in Marxism and "variants of Socialism" a shortcut to development."[21]

---

[19] Par. 19.

[20] Par. 19.

[21] Par. 20.

Also on the *positive* side, he celebrated the "more lively sense of human rights," including the "rights of nations," particularly as supported by the United Nations. In general, he noted, "the center of the social question" had shifted "from the national to the international level." Yet he regretted that "aid for development" had "not always been positive," and that the United Nations had not yet found a true alternative to war.[22]

Year 1989

John Paul began his analysis of the events of 1989 by setting them in a wider geographic context. In particular, he linked them with the fact that "in the course of the 80s, certain dictatorial and oppressive regimes fell one by one in some countries of Latin America and also of Africa and Asia."

He saw this as partly the fruit of "the church's commitment to defend and promote human rights." From all of this, he claimed, "new forms of democracy have emerged," for which he gave thanks, and expressed his continued hope that the problems of peoples "can be resolved through dialogue and solidarity, rather than by a struggle to destroy the enemy through war."[23]

Then John Paul tried to identify the key factors in the recent fall of oppressive regimes. First, he claimed, was "the violation of the rights of workers," so dramatically challenged "in Poland in the name of solidarity." Again, he emphasized that "the fall of this kind of 'bloc' or empire was accomplished almost everywhere by means of peaceful protest, using only the weapons of truth and

---

[22] Par. 21.

[23] Par. 22.

justice." He urged people to continue to struggle without violence and by renouncing class struggle and war.[24]

Second, the pope ascribed the fall both to economic inefficiency, which he saw as "a consequence of violation of the human rights to private initiative, to ownership of property and to freedom in the economic sector," and to the suppression of authentic national culture, at the heart of which was always found "the mystery of God." Continuing in this cultural analysis, he argued that the "true cause" was "the spiritual void brought about by atheism," particularly among "the younger generation."[25]

Finally, he ascribed the fall of Soviet Communism to the opposition's "willingness to negotiate" and to "the Gospel spirit in the face of an adversary determined not to be bound by moral principles." Such Gospel-like struggle, he proposed, required "clarity, moderation, suffering and sacrifice."[26]

In the wake of this analysis, Jon Paul undertook a reflection on the relationship of freedom and sin. "Man," he argued, was "created for freedom," with the result that, where freedom is repressed, society "goes into decline." But, he added, it is also necessary to accept what Christians articulate as "original sin," for in the human reality it should be clear to all that "man tends toward good, but he is also capable of evil." Following a common U.S. *neoconservative* theme, he then defended "self-interest" and linked the denial of original sin with the growth of government bureaucracy and a dangerous political utopianism.

---

[24] Par. 23.

[25] Par. 24.

[26] Par. 25.

*The social order will be all the more stable, the more it takes this fact into account and does not place in opposition personal interest and the interests of society as a whole, but rather seeks ways to bring them into fruitful harmony. In fact, where **self-interest** is violently suppressed, it is replaced by a burdensome system of **bureaucratic control** which dries up the wellsprings of initiative and creativity (bold added).*

When people think they possess the secret of a perfect social organization which makes evil impossible, they also think that they can use any means, including violence and deceit, in order to bring that organization into being. Politics then becomes a 'secular religion' which operates under the illusion of creating paradise in this world. But no political society – which possesses its own autonomy and laws – can ever be confused with the Kingdom of God.[27]

Next John Paul repeated his earlier theme that "Christians, especially the laity, are called to (the) task of imbuing human realities with the Gospel." He praised the "encounter" between "the church and the workers' movement." But he rejected any Christian opening to Marxism, and suggested that the recent overthrow of Communism in Central and Eastern Europe was an important example of authentic liberation for the Third World. He also reaffirmed "the positive value of an authentic theology of integral human liberation."[28]

In addition, John Paul warned of the problems in the postcommunist region. He feared for new flare-ups of "hatred and ill-will," and he regretted that Communism had undermined the ba-

---

[27] Par. 25.

[28] Pars. 25-26.

sic economic virtues of "truthfulness, trustworthiness and hard work. He called a healing of violent feelings, and for "a patient and moral reconstruction." Stressing the interdependence of all nations, he asked for aid from other nations, especially from European nations, but also from the rest of the world, though not to the detriment of the needs of the Third World. Finally, in the whole reconstruction, both economic and moral, he warned of three temptations:

- Return to "the old forms of totalitarianism and authoritarianism"
- Following the model of the developed countries in "an excessive promotion of purely utilitarian values"
- Turning to the "new forms of fundamentalism."[29]

Private Property and
Universal Destination of Material Goods

In this section, John Paul offered a summary of the traditional Catholic teaching on property, plus an extended reflection on "Capitalism" and the "business economy." This section addressed a series of traditional and innovative themes in Catholic Social Teaching. It incorporated novel themes from the *neoliberal* position, but counter-balanced these elements with statements from *traditional* Catholic Social Teaching. (Note that the term *neoconservative*, used in the United States, has the same economic meaning as does the more widely used term *neoliberal*.) The resulting mix of neoliberal and traditional Catholic themes included:

- Traditional teaching on private property and the universal destination of goods;

---

[29] Pars. 27-29.

- The root of these two principles in God's creation
- The new form of ownership of knowledge, and the related skills necessary for business success
- Major failures of the market to include or adequately serve the poor
- The need to find ways to serve those whose needs are not met by the market
- The legitimate role of the market and the business enterprise
- the threat of consumerism to the creativity of the human person
- The threat to ecology as abusing God's creation and threatening humanity
- The family as central to "human ecology"
- The role of the state in regulating the market, and the presence of needs beyond the market
- The general alienation of life in Western (capitalist) societies
- A final evaluation of Capitalism which provided a blend of pro-and-con positions
- The specific function of Catholic Social Teaching.

We will explore these themes under six summary headings: 1) the market and its social consequences; 2) private property; 3) social marginalization; and 4) Capitalism and Socialism; 5) the crisis of the "advanced" societies; and 6) a final evaluation of Capitalism for the future.

Market and its Social Consequences

On the one hand this reflection endorsed, in a way never before found in Catholic Social Teaching, *the virtues of business entrepreneurship and management*. This endorsement seemed to incorporate many of the ideas advanced by the neoconservative (neoliberal)

Catholic theologian Michael Novak.[30] In particular, it responded to his frequent complaint that Catholic Social Teaching repeatedly addressed the distribution of wealth, but had little to say about the creation of wealth. As philosopher Russell Hittinger has written,

> Michael Novak's THE SPIRIT OF DEMOCRATIC CAPITALISM
> (1982) anticipated in some extraordinary ways the broad lines of
> this new phase of Catholic Social Teaching. Indeed some section of
> Centesimus Annus can be read as though they were lifted out of
> the pages of Michael Novak's work.[31]

On the other hand, the statements on behalf of the free market were contextualized by equally strong statements about the limitations of the free market, and by strong calls for significant political and cultural ordering of the market.

This "on the one hand" and "on the other hand"— shifting back and forth between contrasting positions – resulted in a new papal appreciation for "the principle of economic initiative" as part of human freedom, but not in any change in traditional Catholic So-

---

[30] For the work of Michael Novak, see his three most important books in this area: THE SPIRIT OF DEMOCRATIC CAPITALISM, Revised Edition (Madison Books, 1990); CATHOLIC SOCIAL THOUGHT AND LIBERAL INSTITUTIONS: FREEDOM WITH JUSTICE (Transaction Books, 1988); and CATHOLIC ETHIC AND THE SPIRIT OF CAPITALISM (Free Press, 1993).

[31] Russell Hittinger, "The Problem of the State in Centesimus Annus," FORDHAM INTERNATIONAL LAW JOURNAL 15, no. 4 (1991-1992): 955, n. 15. Hittinger refers in particular to the encyclical's "paragraphs" 25, 32, and 35. His suggesting that Michael Novak's thought had strong influence on these sections may be more than idle conjecture, since at the time of his writing Hittinger was Adjunct Research Fellow at the American Enterprise Institute where Novak was also based. I am grateful to Attorney Jay Aragonés for bringing Hittinger's argicle to my attention. (While a law student at Fordham, he provided editorial assistance in preparing the article.)

cial Teaching about the need for social controls of the market nor about the universal destination of all created goods.

Private Property

John Paul began by affirming the traditional Catholic teaching concerning property. Explicitly rejecting Socialism, he affirmed property as a right. But then, implicitly criticizing Capitalism by citing Leo XIII, he declared that the use of goods was not an absolute right but rather was "subordinated to their original common destination." Private property, he claimed, was rooted in human freedom, yet it had "a social function which is based on the common purpose of goods."[32]

The source of the right and obligation of private property was to be found in God, John Paul continued. For "God gave the earth to the whole human race for the sustenance of all its members, without excluding or favoring anyone ... This is the foundation of the universal destination of goods." But it was "through work that man, using his intelligence and exercising his freedom, succeeds in dominating the earth and making it a fitting home ... This is the origin of individual property."

Then he noted that, until "our time" (presumably since the Industrial Revolution), "land" appeared to be the primary factor in wealth. Now it was clear that "work" was itself another major productive factor, and also that work was social.[33]

John Paul further noted that contemporary work was increasingly based on "knowledge ... the possession of know-how, Technology

---

[32] Par. 30.

[33] Par. 31.

and skill." So he recognized a new kind of ownership. Further, "the wealth of the industrialized nations is based much more on this kind of ownership than on natural resources." Thus he praised "the role of disciplined and creative human work and, as an essential part of that work, initiative and entrepreneurship ability" as "increasingly evident and decisive."

He also lauded the "virtues" necessary for such work: "diligence, industriousness, prudence in undertaking reasonable risks, reliability and fidelity in interpersonal relationships, as well as courage in carrying out decisions which are difficult and painful but necessary." (The style here sounds like quintessential Michael Novak.)

John Paul concluded this reflection by celebrating the "positive aspects" of "the modern business economy" and its "basis" in "human freedom," and by again pointing out that "knowledge" had become "the decisive factor in production."[34]

Marginalization

In counter-point to his affirmative reflections on the value of the free market and the "business economy," John Paul pointed out that in the current global market society too many people, perhaps even the majority, are marginalized from any productive role.

The fact is that many people, perhaps the majority today, do not have the means which would enable them to take their place in an effective and humanly dignified way within a productive system in which work is truly central. They have no possibility of acquiring the basic knowledge which would enable them to express their creativity and develop their potential. They have no way of enter-

---

[34] Par. 32.

ing the network of knowledge and intercommunication which would enable them to see their qualities appreciated and utilized.

Thus, if not actually exploited, they are to a great extent margina-lized ... These people crowd the cities of the Third World where they are often without cultural roots, and where they are exposed to situations of violent uncertainty, without the possibility of be-coming integrated.[35]

He also pointed out that others still live in a "ruthless" situation like that of "the earliest period of Capitalism," where "the struggle for a bare minimum is the uppermost." In still other cases, "the land is still the central element in the economic process, but those who cultivate it are excluded from ownership and are reduced to a state of quasi-servitude." "Unfortunately," he continued, the great majority of people in the Third World still live in such conditions." For this reason, the chief problems seem to be acquiring know-ledge skills and gaining "fair access to the international market."[36]

Then, in another juxtaposition of opposing sides, John Paul on the one hand, wrote: "It would appear that, on the level of individual nations and of international relations, the free market is the most efficient instrument for utilizing resources and effectively res-ponding to needs." On the other hand, he continued, "This is only true for those needs which are 'solvent,' insofar as they are en-dowed with purchasing power, and for those resources which are 'marketable,' insofar as they are capable of obtaining a satisfactory price." Further, he added, "there are many needs which find no place on the market."[37]

---

[35] Par. 33.

[36] Par. 33.

[37] Par. 34.

Then, while praising the role of "trade unions and other workers' organizations," John Paul distinguished one meaning of Capitalism from the free market.

He referred here to Capitalism as "an economic system" marked by "the absolute preponderance of capital," against which workers may struggle. Their struggle should not be directed, he argued, at the destruction of the market system, but rather should make the demand that "the market be appropriately *controlled* by the forces of society and the state, so as to guarantee that the basic needs of the whole society are satisfied" (italics added).

Further, he argued, the alternative to "the absolute preponderance of capital" is not "the alternative" of "the socialist system," which "in fact turns out to be *State Capitalism*" (italics added) Rather it is "a society of free work." In this society, he continued, "the church acknowledges the legitimate role of profit, as an indication a business is functioning well.[38]

Then, in a statement reminiscent of what Michael Novak has called a Theology of the Corporation,[39] John Paul reflected on the communitarian dimension of the business enterprise.

In fact, the purpose of a business firm is not simply to make a profit, but is to be found in its very existence as a community of persons who in various ways are endeavoring to satisfy their ba-

---

[38] Par. 35.

[39] Michael Novak, TOWARD A THEOLOGY OF THE CORPORATION (Washington DC: American Enterprise Institute, 1981).

sic needs, and who form a particular group at the service of the whole society.[40]

But once again came several *qualifiers*. First, John Paul noted, "it is unacceptable to say that the defeat of so-called 'Real Socialism' leaves Capitalism as the only model of economic organization." In particular, he highlighted the problem of Third World debt.[41]

Crisis of 'Advanced' Market Societies

In the remainder of this section, John Paul addressed several other "new responsibilities and dangers connected with this phase of history" in liberal (capitalist) society, particularly by its more "advanced" nations. Here he pointed to great concerns about consumerism, ecology, the family, the state, and the function of the Church's Social Teaching.

- **Consumerism.** Regarding consumerism, the pope decried its "direct appeal" to "instincts," while "ignoring in various ways the reality of the person as intelligent and free." Rather, he claimed, the "material and instinctive dimensions" must be subordinated to the "interior and spiritual ones." The failure to do this, he argued, results in "consumer lifestyles" which were often damaging to "physical and spiritual health."

  He lamented that the economic system possessed no "criteria" for distinguishing this hierarchy of needs, and he called for "a great deal of educational and cultural work," particularly for consumers, a "sense of responsibility among producers ... and mass media," and "necessary intervention by public authori-

---

[40] Par. 35.

[41] Par. 35.

ties." He insisted that "the decision to invest in one place rather than another is always a moral and cultural choice."[42]

- **Drugs.** John Paul cited the use of drugs as "a striking example of artificial consumption contrary to the health and dignity of the human person" and "a sign of serious malfunction in the social system." "Drugs, as well as pornography and other forms of consumerism which exploit the frailty of the weak," he argued, "tend to fill the resulting spiritual void."

- **Natural Ecology.** Then John Paul raised the issue of *ecology* and linked it to consumerism. Because these were precedent-setting words, I cite his extensive statement.

> *Equally worrying is the ecological question which accompanies the problem of consumerism and which is closely connected to it. In his desire to have and to enjoy rather than to be and to grow, man consumes the resources of the earth and his own life in an excessive and disordered way.*

> *At the root of the senseless destruction of the natural environment lies an anthropological error, which unfortunately is widespread in our day. Man, who discovers his capacity to transform and in a certain sense create the world through his work, forgets that this is always based on God's prior and original gift of the things that are. Man thinks that he can make arbitrary use of the earth, subjecting it without restraint to his will, as though it did not have its own requisites and a prior God-given purpose, which man can indeed develop but must not betray.*

---

[42] Par. 36.

Instead of carrying out his role as a cooperator with God in the work of creation, man sets himself up in place of God and thus ends up provoking a rebellion on the part of nature, which is more tyrannized than governed by him.

In all this one notes first the poverty or narrowness of man's outlook, motivated as he is by a desire to possess things rather than to relate them to the truth, and lacking that disinterested, unselfish and aesthetic attitude that is born of wonder in the presence of being and of the beauty which enables one to see in the visible things the message of the invisible God who created them.

In this regard, humanity must be conscious of its duties and obligations toward future generations.[43]

- **Human Ecology.** After writing of natural ecology, John Paul raised the issue of what he saw as a deteriorating "human ecology" – threatened along with "natural ecology" by the *autonomy of capital* in the "advanced" societies. He argued that humans must "respect the natural and moral structure with which (humanity) has been endowed," since it is from God.

He noted the serious problems with "modern urbanization," and called for attention to a "social ecology" of work. But most importantly he stressed the role of the family as "the first and fundamental structure for 'human ecology'." Here he described the family as founded on marriage, in turn open to and supportive of children.

He criticized current tendencies to reject commitment, to view sexuality as merely "a series of sensations," and to "consider

---

[43] Par. 37.

children as one of many 'things' which an individual can have or not have, according to taste, and which compete with other possibilities." Instead, he urged, we need to go back to "seeing the family as the sanctuary of life," indeed "the heart of a culture of life," set over against a "culture of death."

In this *culture of death*, he particularly condemned abortion and "anti-childbearing campaigns as a kind of "chemical warfare." This culture of death was the result, he claimed, of "the weakening of the entire sociocultural system" by "ignoring the ethical and religious dimension."[44]

- *The State.* Regarding the state, John Paul reaffirmed the traditional Catholic teaching on the regulatory but limited state. He expanded this teaching's articulation of the obligation of the state to defend the rights of workers to now also include the defense of "those collective goods which, among others, constitute the essential framework for the legitimate pursuit of personal goals on the part of each individual."

- He again pointed out that there are "collective and qualitative needs which cannot be satisfied by market mechanisms." When this is forgotten, he argued, "these mechanisms carry the risk of an *'idolatry' of the market*, an idolatry which ignores the existence of goods which by their nature are not and cannot be mere commodities" (italics added).[45]

- *Alienation.* Because of this forgetfulness, John Paul continued, people in Western societies are subject to a profound alienation. Left only with consumerism, they lose "the authentic

---

[44] Par. 39.

[45] Par. 40.

145

meaning of life" and become "ensnared in a web of false and superficial gratifications, rather than being helped to experience their personhood in an authentic and concrete way." He also linked this alienation to work "when it is organized so as to ensure maximum returns and profits with no concern for whether the worker, through his own labor, grows or diminishes as a person." Such alienation, he declared, is "a reversal of means and ends," and needs to be led back to the Christian vision of "the free person's essential 'capacity for transcendence'." He especially noted the power of the mass media in this alienation.[46]

- **Capitalism and the Future.** Then John Paul returned again to the question of whether, following "the failure of Communism, Capitalism is the victorious social system, and whether Capitalism should be the goal of the countries now making efforts to rebuild their economy and society?"

He responded with a distinction that affirmed the importance of the "business economy," *but he rejected the ideology of Capitalism as an autonomous economic system.* It may be helpful to cite his exact words. After noting that "the answer is obviously complex," he wrote on the negative side:

> *If by Capitalism is mean an economic system which recognizes the fundamental and positive role of business, the market, private property and the resulting responsibility for the means of production, as well as free human creativity in the economic sector, then the answer is certainly in the affirmative, even though it would perhaps before appropriate to speak*

---

of a business economy, market economy or simply free econo-my.[47]

On the negative side, he immediately added:

But if by Capitalism is meant a system in which freedom in the economic sector is not circumscribed within a strong judicial framework which places it at the service of human freedom in its totality, and which sees it as a particular aspect of that freedom, the core of which is ethical and religious, then the reply is certainly negative.[48]

And finally, he argued that the church itself "has no models to present," since "models that are real and truly effective can only arise within the framework of different historical situations." Here he clearly distanced himself from the assumption of many in the Christian Democratic movement that there was a specifically Catholic political-economic program which functioned as a "third way" between Liberalism and Socialism, and from the assumption of many in the certain sectors of Liberation Theology that Catholicism should support a reformed variant of Socialism.[49] Rather, he proposed:

The church offers her social teaching as an indispensable and ideal orientation, a teaching which, as already mentioned, recognizes the positive value of the market and of enterprise, but which at the same time points out that these need to be oriented toward the common good.[50]

---

[47] Par. 42.

[48] Par. 42.

[49] Par. 43.

[50] Par. 43.

But then he balanced that statement with support for workers:

> *This teaching also recognizes the legitimacy of workers' efforts to obtain full respect for their dignity and to gain broader areas of participation in the life of industrial enterprises so that, while cooperating with others and under the direction of others, they can in a certain sense "work for themselves" through the exercise of their intelligence and freedom.*[51]

State and Culture

John Paul's last major section before his conclusion addressed the state and culture. This emphasis on the state and culture, as spheres independent of the market, recalls the anti-Marxist emphasis on three distinct societal spheres, as made much earlier by former Marxist and Harvard sociologist Daniel Bell, and adopted subsequently by Michael Novak.[52]

Here John Paul also repeated Leo XIII's recognition of the three governmental powers (legislative, executive, and judicial) and the need to keep them in a balance of tension. He then described this structure as "the rule of law" and opposed it to totalitarianism, which once again he saw as arising out of the "denial of the transcendent dignity of the human person." He also accused totalitarianism of rejecting the Church, which in turn has defended the human person. Further, he claimed that "the church values the democratic system," though he argued that "authentic democra-

---

[51] Par. 43.

[52] See one example of Daniel Bell's statement of this thesis of distinct spheres, as found in his classic work, THE COMING OF POST-INDUSTRIAL SOCIETY: A VENTURE IN SOCIAL FORECASTING (New York: Basic Books Publishers, 1776), pp. 12-13. For Novak's use of the construct, see his DEMOCRATIC CAPITALISM, p. 14.

cy" is only possible "on the basis of a correct conception of the person." Without that recognition, he proposed, there would be a democracy without values, which could "easily" turn into "open or thinly disguised totalitarianism."[53]

Recognizing that, after the collapse of communist and "national security" regimes, there was a new wave of democratic idealism, John Paul argued that democracy sorely needed "an authentic and solid foundation" in "the explicit recognition" of foundational rights. Here he listed many cultural and biological rights, along with the traditional political ones. He claimed all these rights were synthesized in "religious freedom, understood as the right to live in the truth of one's faith and in conformity with one's transcendent dignity as a person."[54]

Then, in a way similar again to late capitalist neoconservative or neoliberal critiques, John Paul addressed what he described as the problem of the increasing bureaucratization of the "welfare state." He noted many "excesses and abuses, especially in recent years," and he appealed to the principle of "subsidiarity."

---

[53] Pars. 44-46. One wonders here if John Paul may have stretched his argument by claiming that all governments lacking a "balance of powers" are or were totalitarian. Surely there were many historically authoritarian governments (e.g., many monarchies) without this balance of powers, which nonetheless would not have been considered as going to the extreme of totalitarianism. Indeed, the internal polity of the Catholic Church has long had no such ultimate separation of legislative, judicial, and executive authority, since the pope unifies and is absolute in all three. Would the papal form of ecclesial governance then be considered totalitarian? Is this another example of an intellectual temptation to force complex phenomena into the single cause of Marxism? Nonetheless, surely John Paul's concern that modern democracy needs a deeper philosophical foundation than the utilitarianism of modern economism is a much needed contribution to debate on contemporary democracy.

[54] Par. 47.

By intervening directly and depriving society of its responsibility, the social assistance state leads to a loss of human energies and an inordinate increase of public agencies, which are dominated more by bureaucratic ways of thinking than by concern for serving their clients, and which are accompanied by an enormous increase of spending.[55]

Instead of this expansion of the welfare state, he pointed – again in way similar to Neoliberalism – to the role of the Church and the "active charity" of "volunteer work." He described the individual as "suffocated between two poles represented by the state and the marketplace.[56]

To counter this suffocation, John Paul appealed to the wider dimension of *culture*, and he linked culture to *evangelization*. He again addressed the theme of solidarity across the human family, lamented "the recent tragic war in the Persian Gulf," and called for profound changes in human lifestyles "in order to limit the waste of environmental and human resources."[57]

Humanity as Way of the Church

In his conclusion, John Paul returned to the theme of his opening encyclical, REDEMPTOR HOMINIS. He identified "the real, concrete, historical" human person as "the primary route that the Church must travel in fulfilling her mission ... the way traced out by Christ himself, the way that leads through the mystery of incarnation and redemption."

---

[55] Par. 48.

[56] Par. 49.

[57] Pars. 50-52.

This principle, he claimed, inspired "the church's social doctrine," which needs the aid of "human Sciences and philosophy" to interpret "man's central place within society." But, he added, humanity's "true identity is only fully revealed ... through faith" and it is "precisely from faith that the church's social teaching begins." That social teaching, he declared, is also "itself a valid instrument of evangelization," though it properly belongs to the field "of theology and particularly of moral theology."[58]

John Paul then set this teaching and its whole task over against *"the atheistic solution"* found in the Second-World communist societies, and over against the *"permissive and consumerist solution"* found in the First-World capitalist societies (italics added). Against both, he held up "the transcendence of the human person."

He again warned against seeing the collapse of Communism as a legitimization of the present form of Capitalism. He also repeated the theme of the preferential option for the poor, but added to material poverty the cultural and spiritual poverty of the consumer society as well as the marginalization of the elderly and sick, and refugees and migrants. He placed heavy stress on the marginalized, and called for a change in the lifestyle of the others.[59]

Recognizing again that we now faced a "globalization" of the economy, John Paul called for more effective "international agencies" to "oversee and direct the economy to the common good." He wisely noted that "an individual state, even if it were the most powerful on earth (presumably, the United States), would not be in a position to do."[60]

---

[58] Pars. 53-54.

[59] Pars. 55-58.

[60] Par. 58.

In the face of this globalization, John Paul appealed to *"all the great world religions"* to offer "unanimous witness of our common convictions regarding (human) dignity, created by God" (italics added). He added that he was "convinced that the various religions now and in the future, will have a preeminent role in preserving peace and in building a society worthy of man." All this was particularly important, he again reiterated, since we now faced "the third millennium."[61]

Then, appealing also to "all people of good will," giving thanks to "Almighty God," recalling "Mary, the Mother of the Redeemer," John Paul II ended profound and nuanced reflection on 100 years of Catholic Social Teaching since Leo XIII's RERUM NOVARUM, following the recent fall of Soviet Communism.[62]

---

[61] Par. 60.

[62] Par. 62.

7

RECOMMENDATIONS

Toward a Postmodern Pastoral Strategy of
Global Business-Labor Solidarity

T oday in the early years of the Third Millennium of Christianity, Catholicism in the United States (and elsewhere) is
threatened with the same *"loss of the working class"* which so dam-
aged much of Western European Catholic evangelization in the
middle decades of the 19th century.[1]

For this reason, I will: 1) first review the mid-19th century Catholic
"loss of the working class" in the early modern industrial societies
of Western Europe; 2) then explain how a similar threat exists to-

---

[1] The British historian E.E.Y. Hales, in his rich study, PAPACY AND REVOLUTION:
1769-1986 (Doubleday & Company, 1960), wrote that Pius IX (whose papacy
consolidated the "loss of the working class" in much of Western Europe) "cannot be acquitted of some responsibility for what was the greatest tragedy of his
pontificate; namely the failure of the Church, as a whole, to win the affection
and respect of the new proletariat in the rapidly growing towns" (pp. 342-342).

That quotation is cited in my earlier book, MODERN CATHOLIC SOCIAL TEACh-
ING. Part I of that book explores the social and ecclesial context which led to
this crisis of Catholic evangelization with the Western European working
classes. Part II of that book also explores how the implementation of the bril-
liant Leonine Strategy, launched by Leo XIII and centered in RERUM NOVARUM,
prevented the same loss in the English-speaking countries (though it, as noted,
was too late for much of Western Europe).

day in the late modern industrial societies of the United States (and elsewhere across the industrialized world); and 3) finally, make some recommendations for a fresh *postmodern* Catholic pastoral strategy promoting *global business-labor solidarity*.

Western European
"Loss of the Working Class"

As noted, in Western Europe during the middle decades of the 19th century, Catholicism tragically lost the allegiance of much of the modern industrial working classes. One major reason for this loss was an *unjust aristocratic prejudice* by many Catholic leaders against impoverished, exploited, and oppressed workers and their unions.

With this loss, much of late 19th century Western European Catholicism collapsed into to what might be called its *aristocratic captivity*. This class captivity left Catholicism in Western Europe largely without the creative presence of the expanding industrial working classes.

For generations afterwards and still today – especially, for example, in the once strongly Catholic country of France – this *"loss of the working class"* to Catholicism then enabled anti-clerical, secularist, and even atheist movements to gain broad popular support among workers.

So serious did the crisis of France's de-evangelization become that, after World War II, the Cardinal Archbishop of Paris defined that nation as missionary territory.[2]

---

[2] In 1941, Cardinal Emmanuel Celestín Suhard, then Archbishop of Paris, established the "Mission de France," a non-territorial diocese (*prelatura nullius*): *http://catholique-mission-de-france.cef.fr/pages/decouvrez/diocese/introd.html*.

The resulting deep secularization across much of Western Europe still stands today in part as the tragic result of that pervasive anti-worker aristocratic prejudice which so infected many 19th century Catholic leaders, including bishops.

It was not so much that the Western-European working classes rejected Catholicism. It was rather that so many of the Western European Catholic bishops, along with so many other aristocratic clerical, religious and lay Catholic leaders (all largely from aristocratic families) wrongly allowed themselves to become infected by the aristocratic class prejudice against the newly emerging urban industrial working classes.

At that time, many Catholic bishops, and many other Catholic leaders in church and society, viewed the new industrial working classes only as dirty and immoral.

Many of these Catholic leaders became frightened when the workers rightfully protested against their economic exploitation and political oppression, especially in the urban uprisings of 1848. Many of these leaders then supported unjust violent state repression against workers and against their organizing.

Most of those mid-19th-century Catholic leaders were trying to protect the repressive power of the already collapsing Catholic *aristocracy* of Ancien Régime, of which the pope and probably the majority of bishops were themselves members.

A few others, coming from the new 'middle classes,' were trying to advance the rising new *bourgeoisie* through the socially immoral pursuit of pure Laissez-Faire Capitalism.

As a result, apparently the majority of Western European Catholic bishops of that time – presumably, otherwise good bishops – *failed* to establish an effective campaign for evangelization of the new industrial working classes. In this failure, it would appear that– no doubt unconsciously but nonetheless effectively – they *betrayed* their Catholic (universal) episcopal vocation.

What a great evangelical tragedy that so many of those Catholic bishops and other Catholic leaders seemed to be deaf to the Holy Spirit's call to evangelize the poor (*evangelizare pauperibus*, in the Latin words later used by Blessed John XXIII).

Of course, a few heroic Catholic episcopal, presbyteral, religious, and lay leaders chose to become prophetic exceptions to the dominant aristocratic, and also emerging bourgeois, class prejudices against the new industrial working classes. But those individuals were indeed exceptional prophets.

For it would not be until 1891, during the last decade of the 19th century – as noted, more than a hundred years after the birth of the Industrial Revolution and almost half a century after Marx and Engels' COMMUNIST MANIFESTO – that a Catholic pope would *finally* issue a papal encyclical in support of workers and their unions.

As we have seen, that visionary pope was Leo XIII (1978-1903), and his great encyclical was, of course, the famous 1891 RERUM NOVARUM. In that text, Leo authoritatively declared that the Catholic Church supports justice for workers and their unions. He also declared that the Church supports the need for a regulatory state to defend the common good, which included the workers.

For much of Western Europe, however, it was *too late.* Very many in the industrial working classes in the Catholic regions of Western Europe had already been lost to Catholic evangelization.

Contemporary Global Bourgeois Temptation
for Catholic Leaders

Today in the United States, Catholic episcopal, presbyteral, diaconal, religious, and lay leaders face a similar temptation, though in a different historical context, and they are called to a prophetic response which breaks beyond this temptation.

Again, we have seen that many mid-19th century Western European Catholic leaders were evangelically blinded by imprisonment in the *collapsing aristocratic ideology* of hierarchical class authoritarianism, and a few by the *rising bourgeois ideology* of competitive capitalist individualism.

Today, many U.S. Catholic leaders – episcopal, presbyteral, diaconal, religious, and lay – face the historically different but related temptation of being evangelically blinded by imprisonment in the late modern *collapsing bourgeois ideology*. This new and decadent stage of the bourgeois ideology is now *globally anti-union*. It is also legitimating global marginalization of the poor, and intensifying anti-ecological attacks on the planetary biosphere.

Sadly, today some contemporary Catholic leaders in the United States (and elsewhere) have already succumbed to the late modern bourgeois class prejudice. As a result, today many Catholic parishes and dioceses in the United States (and elsewhere) are becoming threatened with *de-evangelization of the late modern working classes,* including its rapidly growing unemployed and underemployed *underclass.*

Increasingly, very many Catholic parishes and dioceses in the United States (and perhaps elsewhere) seems to be threatened with converting themselves into institutions made up mainly of *older generations and affluent classes* – generally all wonderful people, but neither part of the mainstream working classes nor part of its new global underclass.

Also, in this process, a disproportionate number of *younger women* – formerly a great source of loyalty to the Roman Catholic Church – appear to be turning away from Roman Catholicism.[3]

Some may hope that the new Catholic *immigrant communities* will prove an exception to this growing crisis of US Catholic evangelization of the working classes. But the roots of this contemporary immigrant exception no longer seem to run deep.

For, even among Hispanic immigrants (the greatest potential hope for the future of U.S. Catholicism), data is already indicating that Catholic evangelization is *being seriously weakened by the second generation*. Data is also showing that vast numbers of Hispanic Catholics are already leaving the Catholic Church in the U.S., yet not always because of secularization, for paradoxically very many are reported to leave *in search of deeper spiritual nourishment*.[4]

Might their searching be due to an institutional Catholic spirituality *alienated* from the actual social experiences and spiritual needs of the late modern industrial working classes?

In that regard, it is clear from many studies that the *Pentecostal or Charismatic mode of Christianity* has a special attraction for many in the poorer sectors of the working classes, and especially for women within these classes. Yet Pentecostal or Charismatic forms of

---

[3] See Patricia Wittberg, "A Lost Generation?," AMERICA MAGAZINE, 2012-02-12: *http://www.americamagazine.org/content/article.cfm?article_id=13254&comments=1* (accessed 2012-05-01).

[4] *http://alcnoticias.net/interior.php?codigo=20654&lang=688* (accessed 2012-05-01).

prayer and worship are often viewed with suspicion by many late modern bourgeois Catholic leaders.

Hence, the mainstream of leadership within the U.S. Catholic Church – episcopal, presbyteral, diaconal, religious, and lay – may be unconsciously and unintentionally acquiescing in a crisis of Catholic evangelization among the late modern industrial working classes, including its vast Hispanic sectors.

How important, therefore, that Catholic episcopal, presbyteral, diaconal, religious, and lay leaders, appreciate the importance of *workers' unions as an essential mediating institution in the life of the working classes within industrial society, and also as essential to support in the Catholic evangelization of the working classes.*

Abandonment of Commitment to
Catholic Labor Schools

In contrast to the acquiescence by many contemporary Catholic leaders' with the late modern bourgeois global attack on workers and their unions, many prophetic U.S. Catholic leaders during the first half of the 20th century – in faithful response to Leo XIII's 1891 encyclical RERUM NOVARUM – established *more than 200 Catholic labor schools.*

For several generations, dedicated teachers in these schools trained vast numbers of young leaders for the U.S. labor movement. (Similar initiatives arose in other countries.) Many of these labor schools were even sponsored by Catholic colleges and universities.

The blessed fruit for Catholicism in the United States (and elsewhere) was that working-class Catholic families remained committed to the Catholic Church – just the opposite of the tragedy of failed working-class evangelization in much of Western Europe during the mid-19th century. Thanks in part to these schools, during the first half of the 20th Century Catholic evangelization of the working classes within the United States *flourished.*

The same was true wherever else the Leonine pro-labor strategy succeeded, particularly in Canada and more generally the English-speaking industrialized regions – again because in those regions prophetic Catholic leaders embraced RERUM NOVARUM's support for unions (and for a regulatory state seeking the common good).

Yet today, to my knowledge, only *one* major Catholic labor school from that time still survives within the United States, namely the Catholic Labor Guild in the Archdiocese of Boston.

Further, to my knowledge, among the two hundred and fifty one official Catholic schools of higher education in the United States, only *one* Catholic academic institution offers an undergraduate degree in Labor Studies, namely New York City's Manhattan College which recently (thanks to its faculty member Dr. Joseph Fahey) established such a program. If there are more schools with such programs, I will be delighted to learn about them.

Meanwhile, countless state and private non-Catholic colleges and universities have continued to maintain excellent Labor-Studies degree programs. Why have these non-Catholic schools continued to serve the workers' movement, but hardly any Catholic colleges and universities? Why did most U.S. Catholic colleges and universities *abandon the idea of labor studies*? Why did most U.S. Catholic colleges and universities *decide to offer only academic business programs,* and to do so with great vigor at both the undergraduate and graduate level?

Do we have here a perhaps unconscious and unintentional but nonetheless deeply entrenched U.S. Catholic academic institutional expression of the late modern global bourgeois class prejudice against workers' unions?

To make things worse, one suspects that today in Catholic colleges and universities many business-school faculty members and administrators in, and also many senior executives and trustees, implicitly or explicitly maintain the unjust bourgeois class prejudice against workers organizing themselves into unions, including faculty and staff in their own schools.

If all this is true, then a significant number of contemporary leaders of U.S. Catholic academic institutions would appear – presumably unintentionally and unconsciously – to have *abandoned* the once successful papal-inspired pro-labor evangelization of the working classes in the United States.

Instead, in violation of RERUM NOVARUM *and its four commemorative documents, it would appear that these leaders have substituted an imbalanced institutional orientation only to business and not to labor. (I write "imbalanced" because Catholic Social Teaching is equally both pro-labor and pro-business.)*

Again, have these Catholic academic leaders and their institutions perhaps unconsciously and unintentionally collapsed into the late modern global bourgeois class prejudice against workers' unions?

If they have, then such an imbalanced anti-labor institutional bias by Catholic institutions will probably have severe negative implications for Catholic evangelization of the working classes.

Further, if the leaders of many leaders in the broad network of U.S. Catholic schools of higher education have indeed become so imbalanced, however unconsciously, they would also be rejecting an *essential theme of contemporary Catholic Social Teaching.* For, as the documents summarized in this book make clear, support for workers' unions and for workers organizing and defending their unions, is *essential* to contemporary Catholic Social Teaching. And, it is *essential* for contemporary Catholic evangelization.

Without this *essential* part of contemporary Catholic Social Teaching and of contemporary Catholic evangelization, Catholic leaders are threatening to destroy the once vigorous Catholic evangelization of the working classes across the English-speaking industrial world. They are also threatening theological collapse into that heretical bias primarily toward the 'successful' capitalist classes, as once found in some sectors of classical *Calvinism.*

Toward a Pastoral Strategy of Solidarity

Again, the root cause of this above threats is *the recent and growing anti-worker, anti-union, anti-human, and anti-evangelical global bourgeois class prejudice* which for some time has been infecting some Catholic leaders, including in business, education, politics, and even religion.

This anti-worker class prejudice *denies* in practice that workers are *full human beings* endowed by God with *full human rights,* including what Catholic Social Teaching defines as the natural right freely to organize themselves into a union within their workplace if they so choose.

Also, this anti-evangelical prejudice accepts in practice the *false teaching* of modern selfish, competitive, libertarian materialism, which would reduce workers only to a capitalist *commodity* to be manipulated economically according to criteria which do not fully recognize human rights or human dignity as defined by Catholic Social Teaching.

As noted, it is this same class prejudice which has led many US business leaders to ally with the communist dictators who today control China, where workers who would dare to try to form free unions would be quickly and violently crushed by the *totalitarian* state.

Also, it is the same class prejudice which has seduced many other Catholic leaders, including religious leaders, to remain silent while the image of God in workers has been so blatantly denied by the export of formerly unionized US industrial jobs to the communist dictators controlling China today.

Making matters worse, the communist totalitarian government controlling China, because of its policy of forced abortions (or impossible fines) for more than one child, appears directly or indirectly responsible for what is reported as between 8,000,000 and 13,000,000 abortions per year.[5] Meanwhile many Catholic business leaders continue to embrace the communist totalitarian government in China as their business ally. At the same time, many Catholic religious leaders concerned with human life seem to remain silent before this great atrocity.

So the question before us now is: how can Catholic leaders, and especially bishops, creatively and prophetically recover across Catholicism in the United States (and elsewhere as well), the papal pro-union strategy so boldly proclaimed in 5 major encyclicals across 100 years?

---

[5] Apparently, the vast majority of these abortions are of *girl babies*, and also the presumably related rate of *female suicide* in China is astounding. See: *http://www.allgirlsallowed.org/forced-abortion-statistics* (accessed 2012-05-01).

For unions are key promoters of democracy, key defenders of human rights, and potential key partners in Catholic evangelization of the working classes.

In response to this question, I will now make some recommendations for *a new social-pastoral strategy of global business-labor solidarity* based on the following foundational theme of RERUM NOVARUM:

> "CAPITAL CANNOT DO WITHOUT LABOR,
> NOR LABOR WITHOUT CAPITAL"[6]

RECOMMENDATIONS

1. ***Diocesan Business-Labor Ministry.*** Every Catholic diocesan bishop could establish an official Diocesan Business-Labor Ministry, which would be charged with teaching and implementing the pro-business and pro-labor teachings RERUM NOVARUM and its four successor encyclicals.

2. ***Diocesan Business-Labor Advisory Council.*** As part of the Ministry, every diocesan bishop could establish an official Diocesan Business-Labor Advisory Council, to include in equal balance Catholic business and labor leaders. The pur-

---

[6] Par. 19

poses of this Council would be: 1) to study in depth Catholic Social Teaching on capital and labor; and 2) to foster an on-going dialogue between local business and labor leaders.

3. *Annual Business-Labor Dialogue Day.* Further, as part of the Ministry, every diocesan bishop could convene and host an Annual Business-Labor Dialogue Day that would be publicized by an open invitation to all parishes, with the diocesan bishop normally present for the full event. These events would provide public forums for studying and promoting the teaching of RERUM NOVARUM and its successors.

4. *Diocesan Local Business-Labor Liaisons.* In addition, as part of the Ministry, every diocesan bishop could appoint a network of priests, deacons, religious, and/or lay ministers to serve as official Local Diocesan Business-Labor Liaisons to each and every *local central labor council* (or equivalent organization) in the diocese (if agreeable to the councils), and to each and every parallel *local structure for business leaders* (in the U.S. perhaps the Chamber of Commerce or its equivalent, and again if agreeable to the structure), with the appointed persons residing in the geographic area served by the respective councils and structures.

5. *Parish Study-Program on Catholic Social Teaching.* Lastly, as part of this Ministry and essential for it, every diocesan bishop could mandate for every parish of the diocese the creation of an on-going Parish Study-Program on Catholic Social Teaching regarding human work and the economy.

6. *Directors or Trustees of Catholic institutions.* In addition to this Ministry, every diocesan bishop could strongly urge that all Catholic institutions within the diocese, which already include business leaders on their boards of trustees, *also name labor leaders in the same proportion to those boards,* so that the governance of these institutions would embody the full truth of Catholic Social Teaching as found RERUM NOVARUM and its anniversary encyclicals.

7. *Catholic Labor Studies Programs.* Also, in addition to the Ministry, and for dioceses which are home to one or more Catholic college and/ university, every diocesan bishop could strongly urge such colleges and/or universities to establish Catholic Labor Studies programs, perhaps both at the undergraduate and graduate level, with Catholic Social Teaching playing a central role, and with such programs working closely with existing academic business programs.

Were these recommendations to be implemented by diocesan bishops, those bishops would be evangelically witnessing to the *full truth* of Catholic Social Teaching.

They would also be simultaneously laying a firm evangelical-pastoral foundation for evangelizing of the working classes, as so successfully happened earlier due to the pro-labor pastoral strategy of the U.S. Catholic bishops during the first two-thirds of the 20th century.

In contrast to the evangelical failure of mid-19th century Western European Catholic bishops to evangelize the emerging working class, *it hopefully will not be too late* for contemporary bishops leading U.S. Catholicism (and for contemporary bishops elsewhere) to avoid the same failure. In that regard, bishops and other Catholic leaders who do support and promote workers' unions will be establishing their fidelity to the *full truth* of Catholic Social Teaching, which includes embracing the poor, supporting the working classes, and defending workers' unions as *essential*.

The Spirit of the Lord is upon me;
Therefore, he has anointed me.
He has sent me to bring glad tidings to the poor,
To proclaim liberty to the captives,
Recovery of sight to the blind
And release of prisoners,
To announce a year of favor from the Lord.

THE GOSPEL OF MATTHEW,
Chapter 4, Verses 18-19

8

APPENDIX

Excerpts from Caritas in Veritate[1]
2009 Social Encyclical Letter of Benedict XVI

Paragraph 25

Through the combination of social and economic change, trade union organizations experience greater difficulty in carrying out their task of representing the interests of workers, partly because Governments, for reasons of economic utility, often limit the freedom or the negotiating capacity of labor unions. Hence traditional networks of solidarity have more and more obstacles to overcome.

*The repeated calls issued within the Church's social doctrine, beginning with Rerum Novarum [60], for **the promotion of workers' associations that can defend their rights must therefore be honored today even more than in the past**, as a prompt and far-sighted response to the urgent need for new forms of cooperation at the international level, as well as the local level (bold added).*

---

[1] The official English Translation may be found on the Vatican's website at: *http://www.vatican.va/holy_father/benedict_xvi/encyclicals/documents/hf_ben-xvi_enc_20090629_caritas-in-veritate_en.html* (accessed 2005-05-01).

Paragraph 64

While reflecting on the theme of work, it is appropriate to recall how important it is that labor unions — which have always been encouraged and supported by the Church — should be open to the new perspectives that are emerging in the world of work.

Looking to wider concerns than the specific category of labor for which they were formed, union organizations are called to address some of the new questions arising in our society: I am thinking, for example, of the complex of issues that social scientists describe in terms of a conflict between worker and consumer. Without necessarily endorsing the thesis that the central focus on the worker has given way to a central focus on the consumer, this would still appear to constitute new ground for unions to explore creatively.

The **global context** *in which work takes place also demands that national labor unions, which tend to limit themselves to defending the interests of their registered members, should turn their attention to those outside their membership, and in particular to* **workers in developing countries** *where social rights are often violated (bold added). The protection of these workers, partly achieved through appropriate initiatives aimed at their countries of origin, will enable trade unions to demonstrate the authentic ethical and cultural motivations that made it possible for them, in a different social and labor context, to play a decisive role in development.*

The Church's traditional teaching makes a valid distinction between the respective roles and functions of trade unions and politics. This distinction allows unions to identify civil society as the proper setting for their necessary activity of defending and promoting labor, especially on behalf of exploited and unrepresented workers, whose woeful condition is often ignored by the distracted eye of society.

12846751R00098

Made in the USA
Charleston, SC
01 June 2012